Maria Grace's history sheds new light on Austen's writing, exposing hidden n from the modern reads

Praise for Maria Grace

"Grace has quickly become one of my favorite authors of Austen-inspired fiction. Her love of Austen's characters and the Regency era shine through in all of her novels." *Diary of an Eccentric*

"Maria Grace is stunning and emotional, and readers will be blown away by the uniqueness of her plot and characterization."*Savvy Verse and Wit*

"Maria Grace has once again brought to her readers a delightful, entertaining and sweetly romantic story while using Austen's characters as a launching point for the tale." *Calico Critic*

I believe that this is what Maria Grace does best, blend old and new together to create a story that has the framework of Austen and her characters, but contains enough new and exciting content to keep me turning the pages. … Grace's style is not to be missed. *From the desk of Kimberly Denny-Ryder*

COURTSHIP & MARRIAGE
in Jane Austen's World

MARIA GRACE

White Soup Press

Published by: White Soup Press
Courtship and Marriage in Jane Austen's World
Copyright © 2016 Maria Grace

For information, address
author.MariaGrace@gmail.com

ISBN-10: 0-9980937-0-X
ISBN-13 978-0-9980937-0-3
: (White Soup Press)

Author's Website: RandomBitsofFaascination.com
Email address: Author.MariaGrace@gmail.com

Dedication

For my husband and sons.
You have always believed in me.

Table of Contents

Introduction

Jane Austen's books revolve around issues of courtship, love and marriage in the midst of a tumultuous era in history. Her heroines and heroes struggle to find their happily-ever-afters as they wade through a sea of unsuitable suitors, fortune hunters, convenient marriages and social pressures.

But they also present mysteries to the modern reader. Sometimes events in her books don't make sense, like the Dashwood women's loss of their home in *Sense and Sensibility* or Charlotte Lucas's marriage to Mr. Collins in *Pride and Prejudice*. At other times, layers of nuance can be lost when characters follow (or break with) customs that were familiar to readers of Austen's day, leave today's readers scratching their heads and missing important implications.

Join me in examining the customs of courtship and marriage in Jane Austen's day readers and we'll unlock the puzzles of Austen's works and discover her genius anew.

CHAPTER 1

A New Idea: Marrying for Love

Marriage, and more significantly, a marriage based in love was the aim of all of Austen's heroines, but why was it such a big deal? Marriage for love is more or less a foregone conclusion today. In Austen's day though, it was not. More than that, it was a new and novel idea, slowly gaining popularity among the masses.

When the Georgian era (1714-1830) opened, marriages were largely business transactions, frequently arranged by parents and guardians. By the end of the era though, most young people chose their own spouses, looking for compatibility, affection and sometimes even love. But why the change?

Decline of Arranged Marriage

Throughout history, parents used their children, both daughters and sons, in arranged marriages. Progeny were assets in their efforts to gain and maintain wealth, connections, and power. Growing up knowing your destiny is to be a pawn in your parents machinations is such a great foundation for marriage, isn't it?

Luckily for all of us, the Age of Enlightenment (18th century) brought a radical shift in attitudes toward marriage. Ideas of human freedom and equality translated into marriage being a matter of individual choice, not parental mandate.

The idea that a daughter would marry according to her father's choice fell out of fashion, and a man who would force a young woman into a disagreeable partnership was deemed contemptible. The new way of the world was for young people to make their own marriage choices with parents (hopefully) left with the right to veto socially or economically unsuitable candidates.

Or at least that was the theory.

Arranged marriage lingered longest among the upper classes that had the most at stake with respect to money, property and rank in society. Within this group, it was assumed a young woman would learn to love, or at least tolerate, the husband chosen by her father, since after all, he was the best suited to make such a decision for her. This attitude is reflected in *Pride and Prejudice's* Lady Catherine (the daughter of an earl she would have you know) as she and her sister decide that their eldest offspring should wed. What matter that they are still babes in arms at the time?

Even so, few high society parents contrived totally mercenary alliances for their children. Conversely though, not all gentry families permitted their offspring to marry as they chose. Eldest sons, who were set to inherit family lands and fortunes (and who would likely be the ones to provide for their parents in their dotage), found themselves subject to more parental sanctions than younger siblings.

Young women with unmarried sisters (or mothers who anticipated an impoverished widowhood) might also encounter greater amounts of parental intrusion in their marital choices. Hence the pressure upon *Pride and Prejudice's* Bennet sisters: one of them had to marry very well indeed. Without social programs like welfare or social security, unmarried females in need of support would turn first to brothers and sons (including in-laws) for support.

In the midst of all these changes, society-at-large recognized that affectionate marriages based on compatibility were more likely to stand the test of time than marriages arranged purely for material gain. Score one for love, right?

This new attitude complicated matters for parents, though—or perhaps sent them into all-out panic. Now they had to engineer circumstances for their daughters to meet the right sort of eligible men rather than just picking one out for them. The perceived rarity of such men encouraged a husband-hunting hysteria among parents eager to see their daughters well-settled. (Not to mention financially stable, and in an establishment of their own.)

These perceptions were not entirely unfounded. The ravages of war (thanks, Napoleon) and higher male infant mortality rates of the late eighteenth and early nineteenth centuries resulted in an imbalance between the genders. Moreover, the high cost of maintaining a household and the antics of avid man-hunters put young men off the notion of marriage, further reducing the pool of available bachelors.

The Duty of Virgins

Despite the new attitudes of the Enlightenment, one overarching truth remained unchanged. A woman was nothing without a husband. (In truth she was legally nothing WITH a husband, but that's another chapter.)

It was the duty of a young woman to marry. *The Whole Duty of a Woman* suggested that there were three acceptable 'States and Conditions' of womanhood: the virgin, the married and the widowed.

> *Woe to she who remained unmarried: An old Maid is now thought such a Curse as no Poetic Fury can exceed, look'd on as the most calamitous Creature in Nature.* (The Whole Duty of a Woman, 1737)

To avoid that dreaded state of spinsterhood, a girl needed to make a sensible match. What constituted a sensible match? In short, one which provided three key qualities: connections, cash and compatibility.

CONNECTIONS

During the Regency era, everyone knew their rank in society and where they stood in relation to everyone else in their social circles. Unions between equals were expected, and in many families required.

No wonder Sir Walter Elliot of *Persuasion* encouraged William Elliot 's calls and attentions toward his daughter, Elizabeth Elliot. Anne's. early attachment to an unproven Frederick Wentworth was, in part, discouraged because they were certainly not equals at that point in their lives. Later, after Wentworth made a name and fortune for himself in the navy, they became more equal.

Perish the thought of allowing an individual of inferior social standing into the family circle, and thus the social circle. Such an act was considered no less than a betrayal of those within their strata. In *Pride and Prejudice*, Charles Bingley's sisters and his friend, Mr. Darcy, try to use this argument to dissuade him away from Jane Bennet. As a young man, Col. Brandon in *Sense and Sensibility* was sent away from home to the army to break up his romance with an unsuitable woman.

Consequently, especially among the upper classes people often married partners with whom their family already had alliances, or to whom they were related. Marriages between first cousins, neither forbidden by the church nor law, were common. (Aren't we all glad that's changed?)

Misalliances were considered base. A girl should marry to increase her social consequence and thereby her family's. A young woman should never marry beneath her. Matches between men and women of unequal social standing were threats to the rigid structure of society. This was the mistake of Fanny Price's mother in *Mansfield Park*, a woman who married for love alone.

CASH

Connections were not the only criteria. Many titled and influential families were plagued by declining fortune. The lure of a refined pedigree lost some of its luster when tarnished by debt. Consequently, many young men with connections searched for heiresses to shore up failing family finances. Austen's Georgiana Darcy, Caroline Bingley and Emma Woodhouse would be likely targets for such men.

If a young man's family was facing financial hardship, it was his duty to marry money no matter how unattractive the package it came in. Can't you see the lonely-hearts advert now:

Single gentleman seeking young lady with at least ten thousand pounds. Willing to provide an elegant array of connections

How romantic.

This explains some of General Tilney's rage at discovering Catherine Morland's lack of fortune in *Northanger Abbey*. No doubt he was already eyeing the potential contributions she could make to the family coffers when he invited her to visit with them.

In *Pride and Prejudice*, Charlotte counsels Elizabeth "not to be a simpleton, and allow her fancy for Wickham to make her appear unpleasant in the eyes of a man of ten times his consequence." Aunt Gardiner warns Elizabeth that her 'affection' for Wickham would be most imprudent because of his want of fortune . Col. Fitzwilliam notes "there are not many in my rank of life who can afford to marry without some attention to money."

Though young people of both genders were actively warned away from fortune-hunters, the more money and property one had, the greater the burden to make a 'convenient' match. The pressure was greatest on eldest sons to marry a woman with appropriate assets. In *Pride and Prejudice*, Lady Catherine asserts that her nephew, Mr. Darcy,, should marry her daughter Anne to unite the two grand estates into something even grander.

Daughters though, were not immune to the pressure. A young lady of a great family might sacrifice herself on the altar of family duty to help pay off family debts (gambling or otherwise) or establish favorable connections. Elizabeth Bennet of *Pride and Prejudice* faces this pressure when Mr. Collins, the heir to her father's estate, makes her an offer of marriage. (Collins also notes that Elizabeth's dowry is so small she is unlikely to receive another offer of marriage. How sweet.)

As in most things, there was some flexibility in the rules. A wealthy man might be excused for marrying a poorer woman, particularly if she were pretty and had good manners. Hence, in *Sense and Sensibility*, Col. Brand's on seeking Marianne is considered a smart match by the Middletons.

A wealthy woman though, had no such grace in society's eyes. Marrying a man of lesser means, no matter how attractive or good mannered, would be throwing herself away. Thus, in *Pride and Prejudice*, Mary King's family sends her away to keep her from the folly of marrying Wickham , and Darcy, works to prevent his sister Georgianafrom doing the same.

Woe to the plain girl with little fortune, like *Pride and Prejudice's* Charlotte Lucas. She was among the least desirable of creatures. Despite her connections, Anne Elliot of *Persuasion* was in a similar condition because of her father's financial situation.

COMPATIBILITY

Why might a woman 'throw herself away?' Typically, because she fancied herself in love. Corbould (1834) wrote:

> *Most women are inclined to romance. This tendency is not confined to the young or to the beautiful; to the intellectual, or to the refined.— Every woman capable of strong feeling is susceptible of romance; and though its degree may depend on external circumstances, or education, or station, or excitement, it generally exists, and requires only a stimulus for its development.*

Romance is, indeed, the charm of female character. ... (but) It is associated in the minds of many with folly alone.

The idea of marrying for love had gained ground by this era, possibly fueled by the increase in novel reading, horror of horrors. However, a marriage decision based on passion alone was not expected to be correct. Young people were advised to pursue friendship and domestic compatibility instead.

Choosing Wisely

"How wretched must be a woman, united to a man whom she does not prefer to every other in the world. What secret preferences must steal into her heart! What unquiet thoughts take possession of her fancy! And what can men of principle call such an act, but legal prostitution." (Bennett, *1811*)

"Marriage enlarges the scene of our happiness and miseries. A marriage of love is pleasant; a marriage of interest easy; and a marriage where both meet, happy. A happy marriage has in it all the pleasures of friendship, all the enjoyments of sense and reason; and, indeed, all the sweets of life." (The Young Husband's Book, *1839*)

Since divorce was virtually unavailable, marrying the wrong person could lead to a life of misery for both partners. Advice for choosing well abounded.

The Young Husband's Book (1839) cautioned young men to avoid women of bad reputation, low status, those who loved money, or were stupid.

John Bennett (1811) in his *Letters to a Young Lady* offered more detailed advice:

> (T)here are a few general principles of most essential consequence to regulate your choice... **Fortune surely should be considered.** It were absurd to think of love, where there is not some prospect of a decent provision for your probable descendants. ... be as moderate as possible, in your demands of fortune...

> Never suffer yourself to think of a person, who has not religious principle. **A good man alone is capable of true attachment, fidelity and affection.** ...

> The next thing you should look for is **a person of a domestic cast.** This will, most frequently, be found in men of the most virtuous hearts and improved understandings....

> The last thing, though I do not mention it, as absolutely necessary, yet highly desirable

in a person, with whom you must spend all your days, is **sentiment and taste**. *...*

Love, must be preserved by the qualities of the heart, and esteem secured by the domestic virtues... He wants a person who will kindly divide and alleviate his cares, and prudently arrange his household concerns. He seeks not a coquette, a fashionist, a flirt, but a comfortable assistant, companion and friend.

But how did one meet and win such a partner? Unfortunately, the Enlightenment provided little direction as to managing the practicalities of this new way of marriage. New rules evolved to assist parents and their marriage-ready offspring navigate the difficult process of meeting potential partners.

CHAPTER 2

How to Meet 'The Right One'

A young woman's entry into society (and the company of potential suitors) was managed very carefully. Prior to the age of sixteen or so, she was carefully sheltered from the world, acquiring those accomplishments that would prepare her for courtship and marriage.

Becoming Accomplished

Prior to coming out, a young woman was not to call attention to herself. She dressed demurely, often with a deep-brimmed bonnet that hid her face. Young men in particular were not to pay her any notice. She would not speak to adults unless asked a question. Effectively she did not exist in society, keeping her pure and untainted. Exactly the opposite of Lydia Bennet's behaviors in *Pride and Prejudice*.

If her family could afford it, a young woman, over the age of ten, might be sent to school for a few years, but often a governess or the girl's mother handled her education from home. A girl, especially one in the upper classes, required an education to be able to run her husband's household and to be a social asset to him.

Anne Elliot of *Persuasion* spent time away from home at school where she met her friend, the future Mrs. Smith. Jane Austen and her sister Cassandra also spent some time away at school.

To run a middle or upper class household, a girl needed to be able to read and write; elegant penmanship was of course a plus. After all, she would likely be the family correspondent and her letters could be widely read.

She would probably have a book, called an 'every day book', written in her own hand. The book would be a collection of recipes and advice copied from her mother, aunts, sisters, and other sources of wisdom. Passages from ladies' magazines and books might also be copied there. Generations of wisdom (and in some cases misinformation) were passed along in these books.

Sewing was another essential skill, with decorative needlework an added bonus. Women of the era almost always had a needle in their hand if they were not actively doing something else.

As the keeper of the household accounts, a woman needed sufficient understanding of mathematics to manage household ledgers. Gardening, food preservation, an understanding of servants' work and household remedies could also prove quite useful. No time for much sitting around for most women of this era.

To be a social asset, and considered 'truly accomplished', a girl needed even more education. Singing and playing an instrument would allow her to entertain her husband's guests. Pianoforte was the most common instrument played, although harp was considered a higher accomplishment. Her drawings and paintings would decorate her husband's homes. By speaking French and possibly Italian, she could converse elegantly on the history, geography, literature and poetry with which she had been made familiar. And of course, she had to dance well.

The Bennet sisters of *Pride and Prejudice* had little formal education essentially pursuing only what was interesting to them. Although Jane's . and Elizabeth's manners are excellent, neither of them displays the sort of accomplishments that would ordinarily draw the attention of excellent suitors.

Additionally, Elizabeth suffered from a unique dilemma. Girls of the day were admonished to

...be ever cautious in displaying your good sense. It will be thought you assume superiority over the rest of the company. But if you happen to have any learning, keep it a profound secret, especially from the men, who generally look with a jealous and malignant eye on a woman of great parts, and a cultivated understanding. (Gregory, 1774)

Effectively the message was to be smart, but don't let anyone in on the secret. Elizabeth Bennet's wits were considered a disadvantage, especially when coupled with information she might have learned through extensive reading.

The advice rises to even greater levels of irony considering the general belief that girls were not particularly intelligent and could not be trusted with making significant decisions—like choosing a marriage partner.

Coming out in Society

When a girl was deemed ready by her family, she would make her come out. Although some¬time between sixteen and eighteen was the common time for a girl to enter into society, the exact timing might vary depending on the status of other siblings, especially sisters. There was no hard and fast rule that a family have only one daughter 'out' at a time, but, for practical considerations, it was a common practice.

Being 'out' demanded both financial resources and the assistance of friends and connections to extend invitations and make introductions. A family with several daughters might easily be spread too thin if more than one girl were out at once.

In *Pride and Prejudice*, Lady Catherine expresses her shock and consternation that all five Bennet sisters are out at once. Had it been done properly, the drain on the family resources would have been enormous. But with neither parent extending themselves particularly on behalf of their daughters, the Bennet family managed it tolerably well.

Having several daughters out at once also offered the embarrassing possibility that a younger daughter might receive an offer of marriage before the elder. Which was exactly what happened with Mary Elliot, the youngest of the three sisters, in *Persuasion*.

Consequently, younger sisters often waited until the elder was at least engaged, if not married, before coming out. Thus, family and friends were allowed to recover from the experience and finances had time to rebuild before starting all over again.

A notable exception to the practice occurred when an elder daughter had several seasons out without an engagement. After such time, the girl would be considered 'on the shelf' and parents would try again with her younger sister. At twenty eight, *Pride and Prejudice's* Charlotte Lucas would likely have been considered 'on the shelf' and her sisters anxious to have their own come outs.

There was no single established way for a young woman to make her entry into society. Girls in the highest levels of society might expect to come out during the London season, starting around sometime after Christmas. She could anticipate a ball in her honor and an official presentation at court to the sovereign.

Court presentation required a sponsor and a very specific (and expensive) presentation gown and accessories. A whirlwind of society events would follow, all in the hopes of attracting the notice of the right sort of gentleman.

Girls in lower social strata came out with somewhat less pomp and circumstance (and expense). A girl's parents might plan a ball or party in her honor. In Jane Austen's *Mansfield Park*, Fanny Price's uncle held a ball which marked her coming out.

A major event was not necessary, though. A mother might simply allow a girl to begin pinning up her hair (a sign of adulthood) and begin accompanying her on her morning calls and social events to indicate she was out in society. At these events, parents, friends and acquaintances would essentially show her off to potential suitors, for, once a girl was out, a courtship might begin at any time. This was likely how the Bennet girls of *Pride and Prejudice* came out.

Meeting Potential Suitors

Today, one can introduce oneself to a potentially interesting stranger and strike up a conversation. During the regency, proper ladies and gentlemen required a formal introduction, by a third party acquainted with both, before they could interact.

Neighborhood matrons, and parsons' wives, having a wide range of connections, were in especially good positions to effect introductions between young people at social events, both public and private. The Middletons of Austen's *Sense and Sensibility* play this role for the Dashwood sisters. Dinners and parties, feasts, festivals, even wakes, provided opportunities for introductions.

At a public ball, the Master of Ceremonies could conduct this service to enable gentlemen and ladies to dance, though he might not be acquainted with either party. In *Northanger Abbey* Henry Tilney fetches the Master of Ceremonies to introduce him to Catherine and Mrs. Allen so that he might properly converse with them. What a gentleman! This also explains Elizabeth Bennet's horror in *Pride and Prejudice* when Mr. Collins strikes up a conversation with Mr. Darcy, without a proper introduction. His status as a clergyman in no way excused him from the need for a proper introduction.

Though it might seem cumbersome to modern sensibilities, introductions provided a means for young ladies to have some control of social interactions. The men had the power of "chusing whom they may address, and (women) of rejecting whom they may dislike." (Gener, 1812).

Young ladies needed this option since not all acquaintances might pursue noble designs. Not surprisingly, women of fortune were particular objects of pursuit, especially by younger sons not eligible to inherit the family estate.

One such man, under the pen name of 'A Younger Brother', went so far as to publish, *A Master-Key to the Rich Ladies Treasury or The Widower and Batchelor's Directory* in 1742. The book contained a list of London heiresses, their expected fortune and the general location of their residence. The Younger Brother advised:

> *"Thus Gentlemen, have I in the following Sheets I think, opened a fair Field for Action for you; a fine Choice and a fine*

Collection of Ladies; — Open the Campaign directly then yourselves, that my next may be a new Sett. I have one favour to beg of you, and then I take my Leave; that no one of you, of what Degree soever, presume to attempt the Lovely Charmer I dedicate to; as to the Rest, I heartily wish you all Success ..."

Brings to mind several of Austen's less noble men: Wickham , Willoughby, William Elliot.

Alternatives to Traditional Introductions

Not everyone enjoyed success in the efforts to meet prospective suitors. Some lacked the family or social connections to do so. Others simply desired an economical alternative to the marriage mart. For them, matrimonial advertisements could provide the solution. Though some viewed the practice as anything from indelicate to dangerous, men and women from every age group and social class placed advertisements.

Some advertisements emphasized the seeker: a woman of considerable accomplishments and easy independency, a man of respectable rank. While others requested specific characteristics for the applicant: an income equal to his/her own, age not less than 30, no more than 35, an agreeable partner. Meetings might be arranged by a third party or by the matrimonial advertiser him or herself. A single interview might be all that was required to secure a proposal of marriage.

It comes as no surprise that matrimonial advertisements were not always safe. The sensational 1827 case of the Red Barn Murderer, William Corder, involved a marriage through just such an advertisement. His wife, Mary Moore, who met him through an ad in the Morning Herald, discovered he had murdered his previous lover and buried her body in a barn.

Despite the risks, the difficulties of introductions and courtships ensured matrimonial advertisements continued as a popular way to find a marriage partner. Another instance of the more things change, the more they stay the same.

For the more traditionally minded, once a suitable introduction was made, a courtship might proceed.

CHAPTER 3

Nothing is Ever that Simple: Rules of Courtship

During the days of arranged marriages, courtship had been considered a seducer's art. With the new era of people choosing their own marriage partners based on compatibility, affection and even–ack!—love, parents and anyone else who cared about social order and stability had something new to panic about. How did one actually go about courting a potential spouse?

Never fear, enter the conduct literature writers to rescue humanity from itself. Authors readily dispensed advice on how to judge character, attract the opposite sex, behave in public toward the opposite sex, even the proper way to make or refuse an offer of marriage.

Out of this advice, strict rules for behavior during courtship developed. The rules safeguarded both sexes. Gentlemen required protection from being trapped into matrimony and ladies needed to be guarded from becoming attached to men who were not honest in their intentions toward them—because of course, they were not assumed to be rational enough creatures to handle such important decisions without a great deal of help.

Initiating a Courtship

Courtship and marriage were serious steps for middle class men and women, usually not embarked upon until their middle to late twenties, older for men and younger for women.

"The scarcity value of men in Jane Austen's lifetime, together with women's dependence on husbands for status and financial security, gave eligible bachelors the power to act as connoisseurs." (Jones, 2009) Men played the active role in a proper courtship, picking and choosing where they would bestow their favors. So in *Pride and Prejudice*, Mr. Collins' belief that Elizabeth Bennet would be unlikely to receive any other offer of marriage (besides his) accurately reflected the realities of the day.

Women had to wait for pursuit by a suitor. Siblings and friends could be recruited as messengers to alert a potential suitor of a young lady's inclinations, but she could take no further initiative.

Even if a suitor made the first move, she was expected to behave with considerable reserve.

> *ONE of the chief beauties in a female character is that modest reserve, that retiring delicacy, which avoids the public eye, and is disconcerted even at the gaze of admiration.*
> (Gregory, 1774)

A proper lady did not openly encourage a man's suit, hence the scandal of Marianne Dashwood's behavior with Willoughby in *Sense and Sensibility.*

Ironically, refusing unwanted attentions was the one area in courtship where the lady might take an active role. This restricted her choices from among those who made advances toward her. Women commonly felt pressured to accept the first reasonable offer they received, since another might never come their way again. Mr. Knightley expressed this sentiment to Emma over Harriet Smith's refusal of Robert Martin's first proposal, in *Emma.* No doubt Charlotte Lucas felt this pressure when considering Mr. Collins's proposal in *Pride and Prejudice.*

Compatibility, not Passion

Conduct writers recommended young people seek compatibility and friendship rather than romance. The former might stand the test of time and provide far more enduring and stable relationships than fleeting passion.

Young men were counseled not to play with a woman's affections.

> *I cannot even understand how it is flattering to a man's vanity, to gain the affections of a deserving and too credulous woman, whom he never intends to marry. He ought to lose more in his character for integrity, than he can gain as one successful in courtship. ... And to say that he is not bound in honour, because he has subjected himself to no specific promise, is the highest aggravation of his guilt. Were he to act in the same manner in his common transactions with mankind, his character would be forever blasted.* (Gener, 1812.)

Experts warned young women not to give affections too easily.

> *A woman is often placed in a very delicate situation. She may be distinguished by a kind of attention which is calculated to gain her affections, while it is impossible to know whether the addresses of her pretended lover*

will end in a serious declaration. (Gener, 1812)

Discretion in all things

FOR THE GENTLEMAN

Unmarried men had to exercise caution around unmarried young ladies. Attentions or even particular friendliness might be interpreted as romantic interest by the lady or her friends and family. Since men were not to express interest unless serious about a woman, misunderstood actions could lead to accusations of leading a woman on. Pressure to offer marriage might follow. No wonder Mr. Darcy, did not wish to raise the hopes of any young woman in Meryton.

To make matters more complicated, suitors were also advised to take time in courtship.

> *Those marriages generally abound most with love and constancy, that are preceded by long courtship. The passion should strike root, and gather strength before marriage be grafted on it. A long course of hopes and expectations fixes the idea in our minds, and habituates us to a fondness of the person beloved...* (The Young Husband's Book 1839.)

But, attention of such duration could easily be interpreted as serious interest which would raise a lady's expectation. Poor guys couldn't win for trying, could they?

FOR THE LADY

Female conduct manuals universally cautioned women not to be forward in their dealings with men or to encourage their advances. A woman must never confess her feelings until absolutely convinced of his intentions. Some writers went so far as to insist a woman must never look at a man unless he made the first advance.

> *The Advantages of being reserved are too many to be set down; we will only say, that it is a Guard to a good Woman, and a Disguise to an ill One. It is of so much Use to both, that those ought to use it as an Artifice who refuse to practice it as a Virtue.* (The Whole Duty of a Woman, 1737)

Needless to say, it was difficult for either party to truly discern the feelings and intentions of the other. Only at the moment an offer of marriage was made could a man declare his feelings and a woman her own in return.

Following this advice could lead to problems though. In *Emma*, Emma must deal with an unexpected declaration from Mr. Elton in the confines of a carriage. He thought his intentions had been made clear, but she is blindsided by them. An awkward, uncomfortable scene for both.

Charlotte Lucas of *Pride and Prejudice* realized the shortcomings of this advice. She boldly counsels Elizabeth, "...but it is sometimes a disadvantage to be so very guarded. If a woman conceals her affection with the same skill from the object of it, she may lose the opportunity of fixing him; ... there are very few of us who have heart enough to be really in love without encouragement. In nine cases out of ten, a woman had better shew more affection than she feels." Austen's readers were probably shocked at such a proclamation.

Dos and Do Nots of Courtship

Many of the rules governing conduct in courtship helped squelch the possibilities of romantic passion. These included forbidding the use of Christian names, paying compliments, driving in carriages alone together, correspondence, and any kind of intimate contact.

If a couple was observed violating any of them, onlookers would immediately assume a proposal had been offered and accepted. Even mild displays of friendliness could inspire speculations about a possible offer of marriage. Thus, in *Sense and Sensibility*, many assumed Marianne and Willoughby were engaged because of their very open affectionate behavior.

A mistaken assumption of betrothal could be very dangerous to a woman's reputation. Betrothed couples often engaged in sexual behaviors. If a woman was assumed engaged then found not to be, many would assume she had compromised her virtue and her reputation might be ruined. (This was the crux of the favorite romance novel plot point, a young woman being 'compromised') An honorable man might make her an offer of marriage at that point to preserve her reputation. Willoughby's bringing Marianne to tour Allenham without a chaperone compromises her in *Sense and Sensibility*. Running off with Wickham compromised Lydia's reputation in *Pride and Prejudice*. That neither man is eager to marry the lady they compromised reveals much about their character.

CHAPERONES

Young, unmarried women were never alone in the company of a gentleman (save family and close family friends) or at any social event, without a chaperone. Who knew what kind of ideas she or he could get!

Except for a walk to church or a park in the early morning, a lady could not even walk without an appropriate companion. (Of course a potential suitor would not be appropriate!) Though a lady might drive her own carriage or ride horseback, if she left the family estate, a groom must attend her.

Under no circumstances could a lady call upon a gentleman alone unless consulting him on business matters.

In *Emma*, we see the 'close friend or family' clause invoked. Mr. Knightley has been a family friend for at least a decade. He and Emma are allowed liberties to walk and talk and keep company together because of the closeness of their connections. In *Mansfield Park*, Edmund is also permitted the same liberties with Fanny Price for the same reasons. She is family and not considered a marriageable partner in any case because of her low status (being a cousin did not disqualify her from being an eligible match.) Edward shares unchaperoned moments with Elinor in *Sense and Sensibility* because his is considered a family connection through his sister, their half-brother's wife. In contrast, in *Pride and Prejudice*, Elizabeth walking in the woods at Rosings Park with Mr. Darcy, or Col. Fitzwilliam, —with whom she has no such connections—is highly improper.

TOUCHING

Naturally, all forms of touching were kept to a minimum. Sakes alive, what kind of unrestrained behavior might that lead to?

Putting a lady's shawl about her shoulders,

or assisting her to mount a horse, enter a carriage or climb stairs were acceptable. A gentleman might take a lady's arm through his, to support her while out walking.

However, he must never try to take her hand, even to shake it friendly-like. If he did, she must immediately withdraw it with a strong air of disapproval, whether she felt it or not. When Marianne tried to shake Willoughby's hand in public in *Sense and Sensibility* it was really quite forward and even shocking public behavior.

CONVERSATION

Conversations had to be extremely discreet, leaving much to be interpreted from facial expressions alone. Even smiles and laughs were proscribed by many advice writers.

> *There is another Character not quite so criminal, yet not less ridiculous; which is, that of a good humour'd Woman, one who thinketh she must always be in a Laugh, or a broad Smile, because Good-Humour is an obliging Quality...* (The Whole Duty of a Woman, 1737)

Mr. Elton's riddle about courtship in *Emma* is a good example of the kind of roundabout, overtly subtle conversation that could come about because of these rules. And we all know how well that turned out for him.

A Few Good Reasons

Not surprisingly, it was difficult for either party to truly discern the feelings and intentions of the other. Austen used this point to great effect in *Emma* regarding Harriet Smith's propensity to see acts of affection from all her 'loves.'

Only at the moment an offer of marriage was made could a man clearly declare his feelings and a woman hers in return. Thus, poor Elizabeth Bennet was shocked by Mr. Darcy's declaration: "My feelings will not be repressed. You must allow me to tell you how ardently I admire and love you."

Although it all sounds laughable to modern viewpoints, there were some genuinely good reasons for all of the restrictions. While enlightenment philosophy did alter some perspectives about marriage, some things did not change.

At the core, marriage was still a business arrangement. Men and women both brought their assets to the arrangement. Property, dowries and fortunes, trades, skills (including those of keeping house), social connections (of course those might be good or bad, just saying…) and the ability to provide heirs were all very real commodities in the transaction. Equitable compensation was needed for all involved, including the extended families.

In light of all the fuss, modern minds might argue in favor of simply staying single and being done with it all. But no, that would make it all far too easy. During the era, staying single was definitely not a good alternative either.

Society did not approve of the unmarried adult. Spinsters were considered the bane of society, and bachelors were looked down upon as still not quite fully participating in adult life. (Vickery, 2009) A great deal rode on establishing oneself in a comfortable married state.

If this weren't enough reason for anxiety, add to it that divorce was nearly impossible to obtain. Essentially, one had only one opportunity to 'get it right' as it were. Granted, widowhood was common enough, and some married multiple times because of it, but it probably wasn't a good thing to count on.

No wonder parents were in a dither that their children might make a tragic mistake choosing a marriage partner. With so much on the line, can you really blame them for supporting rules designed to keep runaway passions at bay and encourage level-headed decision making?

CHAPTER 4

The Dance of Courtship

To be fond of dancing was a certain step towards falling in love – Pride and Prejudice

In the midst of all the strict rules regulating the interaction of the sexes, the dance floor was one of the only places young people could interact a little more freely. Under cover of the music and in the guise of the dance, young people could talk, flirt and even touch in ways not permitted elsewhere. So dances, public and private, formal and informal, made ideal places to meet a potential spouse and carry on a courtship.

Dance Partners

The dances of the period required a partner. A young lady had to wait to be asked to dance by a gentleman who was formally acquainted with her. The rules governing offering, accepting and refusing offers to dance differed depending on whether the dance was a public assembly or a private ball.

Anyone could attend a public assembly as long as they could afford to purchase a ticket for the event. Both locals and strangers unknown in the neighborhood frequented such events. The Master of Ceremonies assisted couples by making introductions and suggesting partners to those who wished them.

In *Northanger Abbey*, Henry Tilney takes advantage of this service to become introduced to Catherine Morland. In *Pride and Prejudice*, Sir William Lucas often takes the part of Master of Ceremonies at the public assembly. He continues that role in his home when he suggests Elizabeth as a dance partner to Darcy,

While these events offered an opportunity to meet new people, as in the case of Mr. Darcy, and Mr. Bingley, not everyone in attendance might be of the same quality. A young lady could refuse an offer to dance since it was entirely possible that the event might bring her into contact with undesirable individuals.

At a private event, like the Netherfield Ball in *Pride and Prejudice*, everyone was considered introduced, so any young man could ask any young woman to dance. (A young lady signaled her interest in dancing by pinning up the train of her gown.) Unlike a public assembly, if asked to dance at a private event, a young lady could not refuse unless she did not intend to dance for the rest of the night.

Gentlemen, who were generally outnumbered by the ladies, were expected to engage a variety of partners throughout the evening. Failing to do so was an affront to all the guests. This is why Mr. Darcy, was considered so rude at the Meryton assembly. By dancing with only ladies of his own party, he refused to do his social duty and showed contempt for the community. Mr. Bingley did his duty by dancing every dance, with a number of local young ladies.

In general, it was considered disagreeable for young ladies to have to sit out of dances for want of a partner. Silly and melodramatic Harriet Smith (*Emma*) feels the shame of being partnerless so extremely that she values being rescued from it more than being rescued from attacking gypsies.

In some cases, the Master of Ceremonies, or the hostess of a ball, would allow young women to dance together so they would not have to sit out. Mr. Bennet referenced this practice when he threatened not to allow Kitty out unless she only 'stood up' (to dance) with one of her sisters (*Pride and Prejudice*). In the rare cases that men outnumbered women, like at a military camp, men could also dance together with no eyebrows raised.

Not only was being asked to dance important, but the way a gentleman asked for a dance could begin a subtle and powerful conversation with a woman which would not otherwise escape the watchful eyes of chaperones.

The offer might be made with eye contact and a quick gesture toward the dance floor; a smile, a bow and flowery words; a sweaty palmed, stammered request; or even a shrug and an eye roll of 'well, I suppose you will do.' A gentleman might request a dance in advance—a definite compliment to the lady.

On the other hand, saving more than two dances for a particular partner was detrimental to a young lady's reputation. Even two dances signaled to observers that the gentleman in question had a particular interest in her. Observers would consider her his principle dance partner of the evening and all would expect him to call upon her the following day.

Dancing

Balls might begin with a mixer dance in which dancers switched partners frequently, enabling dancers to 'sample' every partner on the floor. These provided an excellent opportunity to scope out partners for future sets, particularly if one was looking for someone of a particular skill level or personality to pair with.

How much can one learn in a fifteen to thirty second set of steps with a partner whose name you do not even know?

Quite a bit actually.

One might meet 'Henry who lists to the left' who leans to the left, does not hear the music well, and is easily confused. Vertically challenged 'Bob the leprechaun' could be all smiles, but unable to count rhythm to save his life or his partner's. 'Dashing Dandy' would inevitably be all too aware of the dashing figure he cuts and ignore his partner accordingly. 'The Colonel' takes himself and the dance very seriously and disapproves of missteps deeply.

Ladies too demonstrated their disposition on the dancefloor. The Highborn sisters, in very fancy gowns indeed, look down their noses at less experienced dancers and effectively put them in their places. In contrast, Lady Congeniality makes it her place to make everyone feel welcome. Miss Ribbons-and-Feathers chatters constantly. Her dance steps are light and lively, when she pays attention to them instead of her conversation.

Whoever might be there, the ballroom floor was lively and full of characters.

The dances for the evening were all built from an array of standard steps. Most of them were simple maneuvers like: partners turn by the right hand and two couples all join right hands and turn once around. Complex movements like figure eights, intricate weaving 'hays' and dancing down the set were included as well.

In many of the line-based dances, couples form groups of two couples who would dance together for one repetition of the music. In simple dances, both couples would perform the same steps throughout the dance. More complicated dances might have the first and second couples executing completely different steps with one more complex than the other, as in Mr. Beveridge's Maggot (featured in recent movie adaptations of both Austen's *Pride and Prejudice* and *Emma*. Ironically, that particular dance was from 1695 and considered old fashioned by the regency. It is unlikely to have been played at a ball during that period.)

At the end of that repetition, the final steps 'progress' couples into new groups of four, first couples moving down the set to be first couple in the group one down from their previous position, and second couples moving up. In order for progression to work, couples at the top and bottom of the line would wait out a repetition of the music and not dance. This waiting out period offered a prime opportunity for couples to interact relatively privately on the dance floor.

In the span of a several minutes-long repetition, dancers might exchange pleasantries, flirtations, or even cross words. Whatever their conversation, though, they still had to pay attention to the music and other dancers so as not to miss their entry back into the dance.

Not all dances offer these 'time out' periods. Circle dances and those done in sets of two or three couples required dancers to participate constantly, so little or no conversation might take place. Even so, a great deal of dance floor communication was possible without dialogue.

Speaking without Words

Eye contact could play a huge role in dance floor *tête-à-têtes*. From a practical standpoint, the eye contact made for a useful way to stave off dizziness from many rapid turns, but it has the potential for so much more. Eye contact might range from friendly and flirtatious to downright intrusive. Some partners, engaging in constant eye contact, could hold their partners in an intense, almost physical grip. Such exchanges could become demanding and intimate, isolating the couple in a room full of people.

Some partners might offer little in the way of eye contact, even to the point of avoiding any direct gaze with their partner. An avoidant partner could silently communicate a variety of things, from their own insecurity with the dance steps to disdain for their partner.

Subtle physical contact on the dance floor, usually restricted to taking hands or joining arms at the elbow for a turn, also spoke volumes. Hands might be taken, barely touching and only as long as necessary, or held reverently, lingering as long as possible in the connection. In moves like passing one's partner in the middle of the line or circling back to back, how close or how far away one's partner remains communicates a strong message.

The way partners dance together creates a conversation of facial expression and body language as eloquent as the finest speeches. A more experienced dancer can subtly and patiently assist a less certain dancer through complex steps with glances and subtle gestures, encouraging and praising with eyes and smiles. Conversely, experienced dancers can declare scorn and judgment on a struggling dancer even to the point of rough pushing or pulling that dancer into their correct position. They might go so far as to gossip about that person's lack of finesse, just in case someone wasn't checking out the dance floor at the right moment to see it for themselves. More than just embarrassing, in the era, to be known as a bad dancer was social suicide.

Partners who are equally anxious about getting the steps right and good humored in their anxiety, can assist one another, laugh at missteps, and celebrate their victorious achievements as they progress through a series of complicated steps. The experience could create a bond over the shared challenge. A gentleman might even kiss a lady's hand after surviving such a trial—a most romantic gesture indeed.

When two proficient dancers partner, the flow of their coordinated movements creates a connection between them, linking them in purpose and action. The communication and energy flowing between them can be visceral and compelling, poignant as the deepest conversation. Compatibility on the dance floor was seen as an indication of an equally compatible marital match.

Each dance possessed its own character, some being staid and elegant and others playful and flirtatious. My Lord Byron's Maggot—by the way, a maggot referred to a catchy tune, what we would call an 'ear worm'—suits its namesake. One set of steps involved a woman inviting a man to follow her with a flirtatious 'come hither' beckon. The three couple dance, Hunt the Squiril (*sic*) requires the first couple to chase each other, weaving through the other dancers. These suggestive moves could be made as token gestures or with sincere energy, all right in front of chaperones. No wonder dancing was so popular.

CHAPTER 5

Games of Courtship

Without distractions like television or the internet, people had to entertain themselves somehow. So, all classes of society played parlor games. What else was there to do during the long, dark winter nights when the cost of candles meant that everyone holed up together in one room in the evenings without enough light for reading or sewing?

With everyone playing parlor games, it was only natural that young people—or those not so young—would make use of these pastimes to their greatest advantage. Games spanned the spectrum from quiet sedate card or word games to very physically active games that could even involve otherwise forbidden touching. Each variety provided opportunities for the courting couple to interact in ways otherwise prohibited by proper society.

Consider how a girl like Lydia Bennet

(*Pride and Prejudice*), Lucy Steele (*Sense and Sensibility*), or even Lady Susan (*Lady Susan*), might make use of games like Buffy Gruffy, Hot Cockles, Move All or How d'ye do? How d'ye do?

Active Games

In **Buffy Gruffy** a blindfolded player stands in the middle of the room while the others arrange their chairs in a circle and silently trade places. Someone claps to start the game. The blindfolded person passes around the chairs and stops in front of one. How one does this without stumbling and falling is rather a mystery, but it certainly does suggest cheating played a big role in the game.

The blindfolded player begins questioning the seated player to determine their identity. The answers are delivered in a disguised voice and with a great deal of evasion. All sorts of touching, which would not otherwise have been appropriate, might occur in the context of trying to figure out the other player's identity. How much depended on what the players wanted to get away with and how diligent their chaperones chose to be.

Hot Cockles took the same notion a step further. In this case, the blindfolded player stood, sat, or most interestingly of all, knelt with his or her head in another player's lap.

No doubt, the Lydia Bennets of the era would push for this version, while any truly attentive chaperone would probably be having a heart attack.

Other players would run up and touch the blindfolded person's shoulder and have them guess who tapped them. The mind boggles at how an enterprising young beau might use this game to their ends.

If having one's beau's head in one's lap, wasn't enough, ***Move-all*** provided the opportunity to have said beau sit in one's lap. In this game, chairs are set out in a room, as far apart as possible, with chairs for all but one player. The chairless player stands in the center and shouts 'Move all' and everyone scrambles for a new seat. A great deal of pleasing impropriety might be disguised under the chaos.

Quiet Games

Others games offered the possibility for people to exchange covert communications as part and parcel of the play. *Emma* contains two examples of such behavior, one between friends, the other between a secretly engaged couple. During the Box Hill picnic, Mr. Weston openly compliments Emma when he notes 'M and A spell perfection.' Such praise was not considered proper and would never be offered in a group setting, but as part of a word game, it was considered acceptable.

The secret conversation between Frank Churchill and Jane Fairfax though was not nearly so pleasing. In playing a game with letter tiles, Frank offers the words 'Dixon' and 'blunder' in the course of the game as a secret message to Jane. Mr. Knightley takes notice of the communication, but does not know what it means.

Clearly, this kind of undercover communication during game play was not uncommon, and possibly even watched for by other players trying to ferret out other players' secrets.

Other word games could allow for very direct statements of feeling while maintaining plausible deniability.

In *'I love my love with an a'*, each person picks a letter and completes the verse about 'their love' with words beginning with that letter. Anyone who cannot fulfill their verse or who repeats what has been said by another must pay a forfeit, more on why this might be a desirable outcome in a bit.

The verses used for this game could be short: I love my love with an A, because she is ardent; I hate her, because she is ambitious; I took her to Andover, to the sign of the Angel; I treated her with artichokes; and her name is Anne Adair. Or they might be long and rather involved—with the potential to be far more revealing: I love my love with an S, because she is sensible; I hate her because she is sarcastic; by way of presents, I gave her Shenstone, a squirrel, a sea-gull, and a sensitive plant; I took her to Salisbury, to the sign of the Sun, and treated her with soup, salmon, sand-larks, shaddocks, and sherry; her name is Selina Smith, and she is dressed in sarsenet. Talk about an opportunity to get a lot off one's chest, all in the name of good fun!

Direct questions might be asked indirectly in a game of **Short Answers.** Ladies and gentlemen are seated alternately in a circle. A lady begins by asking her neighbor a question which he answers with a single syllable. Longer answers exact a forfeit for each extra syllable. For an added complication, neither questions nor answers may be repeated lest forfeits be incurred—unless of course, that's what one was looking for...

With **Cross Questions and Crooked Answers** a little bit of collusion, creativity, and craftiness could result in some interesting declarations. In this game, players sit in a circle. The first player asks their neighbor a question. For example, "What is the use of a cat?" The next player might answer: "To kill the rat, that ate the malt, that lay in the house that Jack built," or something otherwise ridiculous. The answering player then asks a question of their neighbor and receives an answer and so on around the circle.

Here's when it could get interesting, though. At the end of the round each player must repeat both the question they asked and the answer they gave (to a different question entirely). A little scheming could lead to some very interesting statements being made. And if not that, there's always the potential for forfeits if any player cannot recite their question and answer correctly. (Yes, I know, I promise, I'm getting to that.)

Other Games

Still other games provided opportunities for more open flirtation.

In the case of ***How d'ye do? How d'ye do?*** The action allowed for equal parts flirtation, hilarity, and potential wardrobe malfunction. For this game, players would stand in a circle. The first person would begin by standing in front of another player, jumping up and down in the stiffest manner possible, holding their head up high, crying, "How d'ye do, How d'ye do, How d'ye do, How d'ye do?"

The person thus accosted would then jump in the same manner, crying "Tell me who. Tell me who. Tell me who. Tell me who." The first player calls the name of another player, stops jumping, and resumes his place in the circle. The second player approaches the named player and continues the game.

Given that regency necklines could range pretty low and regency stays were designed to offer the bosom like 'apples on a platter', the mind boggles at the possible results of his game.

Just boggles.

Interesting potential of a different sort came in **Musical Magic**, an amusement in which flirtatious actions could be encouraged and even directed by ones friends. In this game, one player leaves the room while the others decide on a task or action they want to see that player take. The action might be as simple like snuffing a candle, or complex like kneeling before another player, removing their ring and placing it on the finger of the other player.

Once the action is decided upon, another player goes to whatever musical instrument is available and they can play creditably well. The first player returns.

That player must then figure out his or her task through the guidance of the background music. The music would grow louder the closer the player got to the next correct action and softer if father away. The music would stop when the player got the action correct.

If the player gives up in despair, which honestly, seems like a likely result, then … wait for it … a forfeit must be paid.

Added Benefit of Forfeits

And now the issue of forfeits and why they might be the whole point of a game.

When someone lost a game, they paid a forfeit. The forfeit could be an elaborate penalty or dare, which might be a great way to get even with one's rival. More often though, they were a thinly disguised machination for getting a kiss. More specifically, the forfeiting player would have to bestow a kiss on someone, often the hostess, but it could be another player. Often, forfeits were accumulated all evening, until the hostess would 'cry the forfeits' and they would all be redeemed at once.

Considering how much flirtation and active courting might be going on under the guise of these games, it doesn't seem at all far-fetched to think that paying or receiving forfeits might be the whole point after all.

CHAPTER 6

Making an Offer of Marriage

Ideally, the rigors of a 19th century courtship culminated in a proposal, called in the era 'making a woman an offer of marriage.' Sounds a bit like a business proposal, doesn't it? Not surprisingly, there were a lot of similarities between the two, including prescribed expectations for exactly how the transaction between the couple would be conducted.

It's hard to believe that Jane Austen's iconic proposal scene between Elizabeth Bennet and Mr. Collins (*Pride and Prejudice*) fit those expectations more or less exactly. But, seriously, it did. Take a look.

Parental approval

In earlier centuries, a suitor applied first to the family before speaking with the woman herself. If her father or guardian did not approve, then the suitor dare not approach the woman herself. But in the enlightened Regency era, such a course was outmoded. Modern society believed young people had a right to choose their mates themselves—as long as their parents didn't veto their choices afterwards of course.

Until the age of twenty-one, both parties to a marriage required parental consent to marry. Even beyond that age, parental approval was highly desirable, but not essential. Since a couple's parents often contributed financially to their upkeep, keeping mom and dad happy was pretty important.

But even where little or no property was at stake, parents of daughters (much more than sons) wanted to be consulted, especially when the daughter was still living at home. In part this was because most considered young women to be ignorant and willful and that they could not be trusted to find men with a good character and sufficient economic prospects. (Shoemaker, 1998)

For a child, son or daughter, to ignore the opportunity of making a grand alliance would have seemed foolhardy, not just to their family, but to their peers as well. (Lewis, 1986)

Pride and Prejudice's Mrs. Bennet and Charlotte Lucas both demonstrate this attitude in their reactions to Elizabeth's rejection of the very eligible (at least in the eyes of society) Mr. Collins. Elizabeth's refusal demonstrates that willful ignorance that parents deeply feared.

Fanny Price faced an even worse situation when she refused Henry Crawford's offer of marriage in *Mansfield Park*. Her Uncle, Sir Thomas Bertram effectively banishes her back to her family in Portsmith in hopes of 'bringing her to her senses'.

And who could blame them their anxiety? After all, what is more frightening than allowing your children to make their own choices and having them be wrong?

Proposals

A gentleman who wished to propose—and it was only the gentleman who could extend an offer of marriage—had the dubious advantage of having very clear procedures to follow. He did have some choices, though. He could offer a proposal in person or more formally, in the form of a letter.

In *Emma*, Robert Martin uses this vehicle for his first, ill-fated proposal to Harriet Smith. In many ways, Wentworth's passionate letter to Anne Elliot in *Persuasion* is also a proposal of marriage.

In either case, it was nearly impossible to conceal his intentions from his intended. An unengaged couple was never left alone, unless an offer of marriage was being made. Similarly, a man did not write to a woman he was not related to unless it was to make an offer. So either way, the lady could be fairly certain of what was coming.

Mr. Collins' proposal contains all the hallmarks of a proper Regency era proposal—even though it makes the modern reader cringe and squirm. Consider:

He secured parental approval.

"... but allow me to assure you that I have your respected mother's permission for this address..."

He, as convention required, recognized her maidenly modesty—a proper woman would never be direct about her expectations or feelings—and treated it as a feminine virtue.

"You can hardly doubt the purport of my discourse, however your natural delicacy may lead you to dissemble; my attentions have been too marked to be mistaken. Almost as soon as I entered the house I singled you out as the companion of my future life."

He established his credentials, including the means he could offer to support her and her future children.

"Allow me, by the way, to observe, my fair cousin, that I do not reckon the notice and kindness of Lady Catherine de Bourgh as among the least of the advantages in my power to offer. ... I am, to inherit this estate after the death of your honoured father

(who, however, may live many years longer..."

And he did not take her seriously when she refused him.

"...it is usual with young ladies to reject the addresses of the man whom they secretly mean to accept, when he first applies for their favour; and that sometimes the refusal is repeated a second or even a third time. I am therefore by no means discouraged by what you have just said, and shall hope to lead you to the altar ere long."

Rejected offers

According to the conventions of proposing, a man should express great doubt about the woman's answer, regardless of what he really felt about his probable reception. This would be a sign of respect, since it suggested that her charms were such that she could expect many worthy offers of marriage. (Shapard, 2011)

While a young woman could refuse an offer of marriage—not really considered a good idea, mind you, but it was possible—she could easily acquire a reputation for being a jilt for doing so. In fact, both parties could be damaged by a refused offer of marriage, so matters were to be handled with the utmost delicacy and consideration for the feelings of the young man.

The woman might tell a sister or a close friend of a refused proposal. Elizabeth Bennet told her sister Jane., while Harriet Smith discussed Robert Martin with Emma. But she certainly would not talk of it to her acquaintance at large, and most especially not to another man.

Not only was it more ladylike to hold her tongue, it might mollify his dignity and prevent him from gossip that could taint her reputation.

Thus, a rejection should begin as Elizabeth Bennet's did, with reference to her consciousness of the honor being bestowed upon her by the gentleman in question.

> *"You forget that I have made no answer. Let me do it without farther loss of time. Accept my thanks for the compliment you are paying me, I am very sensible of the honour of your proposals, but it is impossible for me to do otherwise than decline them."*

This gentle approach to rejection also had the dubious advantage of making it easier for a suitor to propose a second time, as noted by Mr. Collins.

> *"When I do myself the honour of speaking to you next on this subject I shall hope to receive a more favourable answer than you have now given me; ... because I know it to be the established custom of your sex to re-*

ject a man on the first application, and per-
haps you have even now said as much to
encourage my suit as would be consistent
with the true delicacy of the female charac-
ter."

While being very civil, it did make it difficult to make one's true feelings clearly known.
That, though, was in keeping with the general
approach to courtship which largely kept feelings out of the conversation entirely.

Behavior during engagements

Once a couple became engaged, society expected them to act engaged. The couple might
begin using each other's Christian names. Letters and small gifts might be exchanged. A
couple could express some degree of affection
in public, dancing more than two dances together, for example. Chaperones because less
strict, sometimes far less strict. And private
affections might be expressed.

In general, engagements did not last very
long, often only the minimum fifteen days
(three consecutive Sundays) required to call
the banns or as long as it took to draw up
marriage articles. Considering that according
to church records (comparing marriage dates
and dates of a couple's first child's birth) about
one third of all regency era couples went to
the altar pregnant, short engagements were

probably a good thing. (Heydt-Stevenson, 2005)

Secret Engagements

Secret engagements, like that between Lucy Steele and Edward Ferrars in *Sense and Sensibility* or Jane Fairfax and Frank Churchill in *Emma* were considered scandalous moral lapses. Since marriage was the backbone of society, one's marriage state (unmarried, engaged, married or widowed—divorced was not really an option) was an important piece of public record. Carrying on a secret engagement was tantamount to lying to society at large.

For example, once a woman was engaged and her transition to the legal state of *coverture* had begun, if she owned property she could not dispose of it without the approval of her betrothed. But if the engagement was secret, enforcing this was impossible.

Moreover, an engagement was effectively a legal contract, one which could result in legal action for breach of contract. Secret engagements presented a host of difficulties in managing the legal aspects of the contract.

CHAPTER 7

The Price of a Broken Heart

As early as the fifteenth century, English ecclesiastical courts equated a promise to marry with a legal marriage. (This also explained a bit of why so many brides arrived at the altar pregnant...)

By the 1600's, this became part of common law; a contract claim one party could make upon another in civil court suits. (And you thought this was just the stuff of modern daytime television!)

To succeed in such a suit, the plaintiff, usually a woman, had to prove a promise to marry (or in some cases, the clear intention to offer such a promise), that the defendant breached the promise (or the implied promise to promise), and that the plaintiff suffered injury due to the broken promise (or failure to make the implied promise. Don't think about it too hard, it'll make your head hurt.) Luckily, the regency era court did draw the line at actually enforcing the contract and making people marry against their will.

Breach of Promise Claims

A breach of promise suit required a valid betrothal. What constituted a valid betrothal? That could be a little more difficult to discern.

Promises to marry when both parties were below the age of consent were not valid. Similarly, promises to marry made when one was already married (as in I'll marry you if/when my current spouse dies—how romantic!) or between those who could not legally marry were not enforceable.

If significant and material facts were discovered that could have influenced the agreement, then betrothal could be dissolved without penalty. So issues like misrepresentation of one's financial state, character, mental or physical capacity presented valid reasons to end an engagement.

Beyond these sorts of issues, though, the matter was less clear. There was a lot of grey area in what might constitute a betrothal. Marianne and Willoughby in *Sense and Sensibility* publicly flaunted 'intimacies' reserved for engaged people. Those around them assumed a betrothal had occurred or was at least imminent. Marianne probably did as well. This would have been sufficient grounds to pursue a breach of promise suit had she chosen to.

Had Edward Ferrars' honor not been enough to keep him bound to Lucy Steele, she might also have had enough evidence to have prevailed in a breach of promise suit. He did wear the ring with her hair after all. But since they did not act engaged any more than Jane Fairfax and Frank Churchill of *Emma* did, the validity and thus enforceability of their engagement might have been more difficult. Another good reason why secret engagements were so strongly frowned upon.

If a betrothal was valid, a breach of promise claim could be presented in court.

Why Sue for Breach of Promise?

Why were such claims filed when it seems like it would be far easier, less painful and less embarrassing for a couple to simply go their separate ways? If it were only hurt feelings on the line, that's probably what would have happened. But, when a promise to marry was broken, the rejected party, usually female, suffered both social and economic losses.

Socially, an engaged couple was expected to act like an engaged couple. It seems unfair in modern eyes, but the behaviors she may have shared with her betrothed, (remember the bit about a promise to marry being essentially equivalent to being married?) would leave her reputation damaged if he left her.

Though premarital sex was officially frowned upon, it was known that a woman was much more likely to give up her virginity under a promise to marry. If that promise was not kept, her future search for a husband would be significantly hampered for having broken the accepted code of maidenly modesty.

The loss of reputation translated to serious economic losses, since middle and upper class women did not work outside the home and required a household supported by a husband's wealth. A woman with a tarnished reputation was unlikely to marry well.

If she or her family had spent money on clothes or the like in the anticipation of the marriage, those expenses were considered among the damages as well. Although less common, a man who sued for breach of promise could also include expenses related to the relationship as part of the damage claim.

It really does sound like reality TV- regency edition, doesn't it?

Damage Awards

Perhaps as a result of the real long-term damage a woman might suffer from a broken engagement, a woman was far more likely to win a breach of promise claim than lose one. Of the 2395 cases filed by women between 1780 and 1939, only 274 women lost. Only 75 men filed such claims in the same time period with only 42 winning their case. (Bates, 2016)

Middle-class ladies were generally able to obtain larger damage awards than working class women (they were 'worth' more, after all), though cases varied greatly. About half of women who won damages obtained £50 - £200. (Bates, 2016) (For reference, a middle class family of four could live comfortably on £250 a year.)

While these awards could indeed offer assistance to wronged plaintiffs, the system was also ripe for abuse. Jurors were often unduly sympathetic toward jilted women, especially when they were attractive or portrayed as particularly virtuous. Damage awards could easily be swayed by such sympathies, making false claims very tempting.

All this sounds so very modern, doesn't it? The more things change, the more they stay the same!

CHAPTER 8

Show Me the Money

Prenuptial agreements s might seem like a relatively new addition to the marriage landscape, however, they've been in existence for centuries. While today they often include provisions for how properties will be separated in the event of a marriage ending, during the regency era that wasn't even a consideration. Except by an act of Parliament (literally), marriages only ended in death.

Drafting prenuptial agreements was expensive, though, costing around £100, so only about ten percent of marriages actually were covered by marriage settlements. The agreements focused on how the value each individual brought into the marriage would be distributed in both the immediate and more distant future.

These provisions were necessary because a woman's legal position changed dramatically at marriage. Her existence as a legal individual effectively disappeared and her husband assumed the legal existence for both of them.

Women's Legal Position

In 1765, William Blackstone presented a common man's language interpretation of English law. He explains the law's approach to women's legal existence and rights in marriage which remained largely unchanged until the Married Women's Property Act of 1884.

Blackstone said:

> *By marriage, the husband and wife are one person in law: that is, the very being or legal existence of the woman is suspended during the marriage, or at least is incorporated and consolidated into that of the husband... and her condition during her marriage is called her coverture.*

> *... For this reason, a man cannot grant anything to his wife, or enter into covenant with her: for the grant would be to suppose her separate existence; and to covenant with her, would be only to covenant with himself: ... a husband may also bequeath anything to his wife by will; for that cannot take effect till the coverture is determined by his death.*

> *... the chief legal effects of marriage during the coverture; upon which we may observe, that even the disabilities which the wife lies*

> *under are for the most part intended for her*
> *protection and benefit: so great a favourite*
> *is the female sex of the laws of England.*

Effectively this common law doctrine rendered married women unable to sign bills of exchange, make contracts, buy property, write a will, act as a business partner, own her own earnings or have custody of her children. I'm not sure the law favored women the way Blackstone thought it did.

Ironically, single women and widows were able to act with much greater independence. In many cases widowhood gave a woman the greatest legal freedoms, which many wealthy widows were loath to give up by remarrying.

It was not until the Married Women's Property Act of 1884 that married women enjoyed the same legal rights as unmarried women.

Marriage Settlements

In most cases, women did not bring a great deal of property or money into a marriage (of course, neither did the husband). When there was substantial property involved, legal documents called marriage settlements or articles were required by one or both families.

A marriage settlement was a prenuptial agreement (bet you thought that was a modern invention!) that established the financial terms of the marriage. The terms included stipulations about what was to be done with the wife's dowry, what her discretionary income would be (known as 'pin money'), what her income would be if she became a widow, and what total amount would go to her children—male and female—from the monies she brought into the marriage. The timing of these payments was also often specified.

Parents could also 'settle' money on the couple in the marriage articles. Jane Austen references this in Lydia's settlement with Wickham in which Mr. Bennet is to allow her £100 per year during his lifetime.

A Woman's Dowry

Though Mr. Bennet referred to dowries as bribes to worthless young men to marry his daughters, dowries were more commonly considered a means by which a responsible family compensated a husband for their daughter's lifelong upkeep. How's that for a romantic notion?

Dowries (or more commonly the interest earned off a dowry) were used to provide a woman's lifetime spending money, set her income if she became a widow, and eventually distributed to her children at the death of one or both parents.

Settlements specified a total amount of

money set aside for daughter's dowries. The more daughters a family had, the more ways the sum would have to be divided. The division of the money was generally not specified, so it did not have to be divided evenly amongst the daughters. A father might add to the sum during his lifetime, but if not stipulated in the settlement, it was not required. So the five Bennet daughters had to divide their mother's five thousand pound dowry among them, with nothing added by their father.

There was no guarantee that a woman's family would have the cash on hand to pay a dowry upon marriage. Oftentimes, that sum was tied up in estate capital or investments. The family might have to take out a mortgage to pay the dowry, or a down payment on it, with the final portion due from the estate at the father's death.

To replenish the loss of capital, the heir of the estate needed to marry a bride with her own fortune. Marrying a woman without sufficient capital could harm the financial position of the family estate. For Mr. Darcy, of *Pride and Prejudice*, his sister, Georgiana's, considerable fortune of £30,000 would come out of the Pemberley coffers on her marriage. By choosing a bride who could not replenish that, Darcy, was putting Pemberley's financial future at risk.

The Special Case of Separate Estates

Women like Georgiana Darcy or even Caroline Bingley who had outrageous amounts of money in their dowries, Anne de Bourgh who owned real property, or widows who inherited large fortunes from their late husbands, like Lady Russell (*Persuasion*) might wish to protect their fortunes since at marriage (or remarriage) EVERYTHING would belong to their husbands and she had no further rights to it.

(Technically, there was one exception. Wedding presents and "paraphernalia"— clothing and jewelry—given by friends or family were considered the wife's property.) (Laudermilk, 1989)

As early as 1620, trusts were used to create separate estates (though the term was not used in the era) that would prevent a husband from accessing his wife's property. (Marriage Settlements, 2009) All the protected assets would be placed in the trust, prior to the marriage, and trustees appointed to administer the trust. Through the trustees, a woman could draw her own income from the trust, access the contents of the trust, and ensure that its future disposition was according to her wishes. In some cases, the husband could be named trustee. But, he would be bound by the terms of the trust and would answer to the Chancery

Court which oversaw the terms of the trusts.

Trusts could contain both money and real property like shipping fleets, mills, landed estates, even unset gemstones. (Laudermilk, 1989)

Separate property also protected a woman's assets from her husband's creditors. Her property could not be seized and sold off to pay her husband's debts. Not surprisingly, heiresses and other women of wealth were strongly dissuaded from protecting their property in this way because it showed a decidedly unromantic distrust in their future husbands.

How romantic.

Contents of the Marriage Settlement

PIN MONEY

Pin money, a woman's disposable income, was stipulated in the marriage settlement. It represented money she could spend without answering to her husband. Since common law only stipulated that a man had to provide his wife's 'necessities', pin money could supply the 'luxuries' that might be required to live the lifestyle to which she was accustomed.

The concept makes a great deal of sense, but since only a small minority of women enjoyed marriage settlements, most probably did not enjoy the luxury of their own private allowance to be spent as they wished. Mrs.

Bennet of *Pride and Prejudice* gushes over the pin money she expects daughters Jane . and Elizabeth to have as a consequence of marrying wealthy men. Later, Elizabeth notes making gifts to sister Lydia out of that pin money instead of bringing Lydia's requests for support to her husband.

DOWER AND JOINTURE

Until into the nineteenth century, without a jointure in a pre-marital contract, English common law ensured the widow had a right to a life interest in one third of the freehold lands in her husband's hands at the time of her marriage. The only way the widow could lose these rights was if her husband or herself was found guilty of treason, felony or adultery.

The jointure, the settlement on a bride by her future husband of a freehold estate secured for her widowhood, came into practice with the Statute of Uses (1535). To receive this settlement, the prospective wife had to surrender her dower (not to be confused with her dowry which was something different altogether.)

With formal repeal of dower in 1833, wives lost the absolute right to inherit. So in the absence of jointure provisions or explicit provisions in a husband's will, the widow could be left without support at her husband's death. If a man left his wife property upon his death, it might be marked with the stipulation that it would revert to his heir or another designate if she remarried.

Jointures were rarely on the same level as the dowry a woman brought to the marriage. They were usually anchored on the amount that a woman brought into a marriage. Generally it was an annuity, payable by the heir of the estate, equal to one tenth of a woman's dowry. The annuity would be payable by the heir of a man's estate until the woman's death upon which time the principle would descend to her children.

The ratio of jointure to dowry was established by the expectation that the average wife would outlive her husband by about ten years. Thus, she would most likely receive back the amount she brought into the marriage over the duration of her widowhood.

The issues of jointure and inheritance created the initial problems for the widowed Mrs. Dashwood and her daughters in *Sense and Sensibility*. Mrs. Dashwood was the second wife of Mr. Dashwood and not the mother of his heir (his son). The estate passed into his son's hands at the senior Mr. Dashwood's death.

Since the current Mrs. Dashwood was not the heir's mother, he had no obligation to provide for her or her daughters--and did not deign to do so. Instead, the widow and her daughters were forced to live on the income supplied by the jointure, £500. (This implies that she brought £5000 into the marriage as her dowry.) While the amount is sufficient to maintain them, it is not enough for luxuries like a carriage which would generally require twice that income to support.

SETTLEMENTS TO THE CHILDREN

Marriage settlements also stipulated provisions for a couple's children. Special provisions for children from a prior marriage would be included to insure that they received portions from their father's property if it was in their mother's hands at the time of her re-marriage. If a man were widowed, these same provisions protected a first wife's children from losing their mother's fortune to a subsequent wife's machinations. Those terms might also limit what a father could pass down to children from subsequent wives, the case in *Sense and Sensibility*.

The monies a woman brought into the marriage through her dowry and any other settlements on her, would go to her children, both sons and daughters, upon her death. Additional funds could be settled on the children from the father's estate. The marriage articles would stipulate the amounts.

Typically, only the total amounts would be set forth in the settlement, not the division among the children. This made sense given there was no way to know ahead of time how many children of which gender would be born. One consequence, though, was that a parent might threaten to readjust the division of the funds in order to control the behavior of a child set on thwarting his or her parent's wishes. Mrs. Ferrars in *Sense and Sensibility* did this when Edward refused to give up Lucy Steele. She settled her fortune irrevocably upon his younger brother—who of course then took up with Lucy Steele himself. Clever girl.

While all these documents and legal requirements make for great plot points in fiction, it is important to remember most women would have been happy with a dowry of a few hundred pounds; most children did not inherit vast sums or property from their parents; and most widows had to rely on their children and other family for support.

CHAPTER 9

Licenses, Laws and the Legalities of Getting Married

Engagements in the regency era were generally brief, often only a few weeks long. Since premarital sex was common and the birth of illegitimate children problematic for inheritance, there was considerable pressure to see couples married sooner rather than later.

If there was property or fortune involved, a couple had to wait for marriage articles to be drawn, a process that could take weeks or months depending on the difficulty of establishing an agreeable settlement. Otherwise, they only need wait to fulfill the requirements of legal marriage.

Reading the banns or acquiring a license and having the marriage performed required a minimum of fifteen days to accomplish.

The Hardwicke Marriage Act of 1753

Before 1754, marriage in England and Wales was governed by canon law of the Church of England, not civil law. This led to some confusion about what exactly constituted a marriage.

While canon law recommended reading banns or acquiring a marriage license, the only absolute requirement was that the marriage be solemnized by an Anglican clergyman. Even so, many believed that the exchange of consent by parties of sufficient age (fourteen for men and twelve for women) in front of two witnesses made a marriage. This led to a great deal of misunderstanding about which marriages were actually valid and proved a record keeping nightmare.

Witnesses had to be produced to validate claims of marriage. Witnesses of the era were no more reliable (or honest) than witnesses today. Their testimonies could be altered by personal agendas or bribes, potentially leaving individuals suddenly married or unmarried and children made illegitimate.

With fortunes, property and family names on the line, the courts found the situation intolerable. Thus, the introduction of "An Act for the Better Preventing of Clandestine Marriage", known as Lord Hardwicke's Marriage Act or The Marriage Act of 1753. It came into force on March 25, 1754. (See Appendix C)

The Act stipulated couples must purchase a

license or have banns read during three consecutive church services. These stipulations were intended to ensure that the couple was eligible to marry.

Couples under twenty one years of age required parental consent to marry by license. Underage couples could marry by banns as long as the minor's parents did not forbid the banns.

Finally the marriage must be conducted between the hours of 8AM and noon, before witnesses, in a church, by authorized clergy and duly recorded in a marriage register. The later provided definitive proof the marriage occurred.

There were some exemptions to the marriage act: the royal family, Jews and Quakers (though the Act did not actually declare Jewish and Quaker marriages legal either.) Catholics though, were not exempt. Any marriage performed according to Catholic rites had to be repeated by clergy of the Church of England in order to be a valid marriage.

Marriage by Banns

Most couples married by publishing the banns. The process cost little to nothing and took about three weeks. Harriet Smith of Jane Austen's Emma would likely have married this way.

To publish the banns, the local clergyman would, on three consecutive Sundays announce: "I publish the Banns of marriage *between Groom's Name of–his local parish–and Bride's Name of–her local parish.* If any of you know cause or just impediment why these two persons should not be joined together in Holy matrimony, ye are to declare it. This is the first [second or third] time of asking."

If someone objected to the marriage, they would go directly to the clergyman to provide evidence to support their objections. Relevant objections might include: one party was otherwise married, engaged to be married, or inappropriately related to the other, or a parent might object if one was under age.

Naturally people could, and did present other objections. Relatives might not like the choice of spouse, old grudges might come to light. Sometimes people did not wait to bring it up privately, but called it out during the reading of the banns themselves, resulting in rather memorable holy services. Sounds like fodder for today's daytime television, doesn't it?

It was little wonder that the wealthy and well connected disliked the public aspect of reading banns.

After the banns were called three times, with no objections, the couple had ninety days in which to marry, otherwise the banns would have to be called again.

If bride and groom lived in different church parishes, the banns had to be read in both of their parishes. If the banns were thrice called without objection, the local clergyman would produce a certificate attesting to the fact to be presented to the clergyman performing the wedding ceremony.

Marriage by License

Those wishing greater privacy, speed, flexibility or prestige could purchase a license for marriage instead of having banns read. An ordinary license was less expensive, though still out of reach for many. A special license was reserved for the wealthiest elite who could afford it. Either form of license required a sworn 'allegation' giving assurances that no official impediments to the marriage existed.

COMMON OR ORDINARY LICENSE

Common or ordinary licenses were issued by archbishops, bishops, and some archdeacons, or by clergy in certain parishes. These licenses permitted a marriage to take place within fifteen days in one of the parishes named on the license (either one of the couple's resident parishes or one in which at least one of them had resided in for a minimum of fifteen days.) Weddings still had to take place in a church, by an Anglican clergyman, between 8 AM and noon, and be entered in the official marriage register. This is the type of license Mr. Darcy, of *Pride and Prejudice* would have purchased for Wickham to marry Lydia.

Mrs. Bennet hopes for something better for her elder daughters with their wealthy betrotheds. Perhaps they might marry by special license.

SPECIAL LICENSE

> *"The privilege (of a special license) was only granted to a limited aristocratic cadre: Peers and Peeresses in their own right, to their sons and daughters, to Dowager Peeresses, to Privy Councilors, to Judges of the Courts at Westminster, to Baronets and Knights, and to Members of Parliament. Others could be granted a (special) license, if they could allege very strong and weighty reasons for such indulgence, arising from particular circumstances of the case, the truth of which must be proved to the satisfaction of the Archbishop (of Canterbury). In practice these requirements were sometimes interpreted with some liberality."*
> (Rogers, 2006)

Special licenses enabled people to be married outside a church or chapel. Couples might select a fashionable location or a private home. Weddings could also be conducted outside the hours of 8AM to noon. While a few of

Jane Austen's characters might have been able to acquire a special license, it seems unlikely that any of them actually did.

Relatives Forbidden to Marry

Close relatives were forbidden to marry by laws of consanguinity. Although a long, detailed list of such close relations could be found in the Book of Common Prayer, (see Appendix B) the rules could be summed up as: a person may not wed their own sons/daughters, siblings, parents, aunts/ uncles, nieces/nephews, grandparents, or grandchildren, whether the relationship was by blood, half blood or marriage.

This got a little sticky when a widowed man wanted to marry his deceased wife's sister. Often times when a woman died, her sister stepped in to fill her role in the household, especially when there were children involved. So the issue was not at all uncommon.

There was no outright ban on these marriages until 1835, but they were problematic. The marriages were considered voidable, that is they could be annulled by either party and the children of the marriage declared illegitimate. It was not until 1907 that marrying a deceased wife's sister became legal and 1921 that marrying a deceased husband's brother became legal.

Cousin unions, on the other hand, were allowed, in any degree. Especially among the landed classes, their ability to unite estates and increase family wealth made them highly acceptable. So in *Pride and Prejudice*, Lady Catherine's hopes for her daughter Anne to marry cousin Mr. Darcy, were not at all problematic for the era. . Similarly, Mr. Collins was free to pursue any of his lovely cousins, the Bennet sisters and William Elliot was free to seek the hand of either of the unmarried Elliot sisters in *Persuasion*.

In contrast though, "lower down the social scale, where reasons of estates were less applicable and where people also had far more potential mates to choose among, marriage between first cousins was more likely to be regarded as incestuous. (Shapard, 2003)

CHAPTER 10

Why not Elope?

What could be more romantic than a couple so in love they could not wait to be married and eloping to Gretna Green for an immediate marriage? Certainly Lydia Bennet of *Pride and Prejudice* would have agreed.

But she would have been wrong. Very wrong.

Turns out, eloping could cause quite a bit of trouble, including bringing the legality of the marriage and legitimacy of the children from such a marriage into question. It also put a young woman, especially one with a fortune, in a dangerous position. If the marriage was considered legitimate, her fortune would be irrevocably in the hands of her husband and she would have no guaranteed provision for her or her children's future. If it was not, her reputation would be ruined and her chances of making a good marriage possibly gone forever. Not exactly a win-win proposition.

If it could cause so much trouble, why would anyone consider it an option? In short, it was a way around the limitations created by the Hardwicke Act.

Why Elope

If a couple was considering eloping, parental consent was usually the fly in the ointment. If a woman (or man, but that was less likely) was too young, and her guardian would not consent, as in the case of Georgiana Darcy, and George Wickham in *Pride and Prejudice*, the couple would have to wait until she was twenty-one to marry. Eloping provided a quicker way to marital bliss.

Sometimes, the reading of the banns might raise an objection. Perhaps one of the parties was promised to marry another, or worse, had already married another. Either could put a crimp on a young couple's plans. Purchasing a license instead of reading the banns might provide a way to work around this, but since the "standard license from a bishop required a bond for £100 to be forfeit if the couple lied" (Mayer, Marriage) about any pertinent detail, the option was not open to many.

The case of Julia Bertram from *Mansfield Park* offers a completely different reason to elope. In her case, she elopes immediately after her sister Maria's shameful abandonment of her husband for Henry Crawford. Maria's actions were so egregious they could permanently ruin her standing in society.

The stain might easily extend to Julia as well, possibly ruining her chance for a good match. Thus, she elopes, whether to attain a good match before it becomes impossible or just to avoid getting blamed for Maria's misdeed, the reader is left to decide for themselves.

Was it a favorable match? Julia elopes with The Honorable John Yates, who had been pursuing her since their introduction. Although the book doesn't tell us much about Yates, his title reveals he is the son of a peer, and thus, not an entirely inappropriate match for the daughter of a baronet. So that is some good news for the poor girl.

The Allure of Gretna Green

With the stipulations of the Hardwicke Act in place, how did a couple manage an elopement?

An obvious solution might be to go somewhere the Hardwicke Act didn't apply to get married, like perhaps Scotland. Scottish law merely required two witnesses and a minimum age of sixteen for both parties. (Of course for now, we'll ignore the fact that whether or not Scottish marriages were legally valid in England was a matter of some debate.)

Gretna Green was just nine miles from the last English staging post at Carlisle and just one mile over the Scottish border. The town took advantage of the situation and made something of a business in quick marriages, not unlike Las Vegas today. Hence, it was known for elopements and it became a favorite plot device for romance writers everywhere.

If it was so simple and convenient, why not go to Gretna Green to marry? Barring the fact that elopements were a good way to get ostracized from good society, there were practical considerations that made it unsuitable for many.

Gretna Green is three hundred twenty miles from London, the largest British population center of the early 1800's. My local highways boast an eighty or eighty five mile per hour speed limit, so I can travel that distance in half a day, no bother. In the early 1800's those speeds were unheard of. Most people walked. Everywhere. Only the very wealthy had horses and carriages of their own.

If one were moderately well off, they might purchase tickets on a public conveyance to go long distances. While better than walking, one could still only expect to travel five to seven miles per hour. Traveling twelve hours a day, with only moderate stops to change horses and deal with personal necessities, the trip would take about four days.

Four days packed in a jolting, swaying carriage with as many other people as the proprietors could squeeze into the space and more sitting on top of the coach.

A lovely, romantic picture, yeah?

If a couple was wealthy enough to enjoy a private conveyance, they might not have to share the coach with others, but little if any time could be shaved off the trip.

Luckily, Gretna Green was not the only option. Other locations were available to facilitate a clandestine marriage. Towns along the eastern borders of Scotland, like Lamberton, Paxton, Mordington and Coldstream also catered to eloping couples. In some cases, the toll-keepers along the road officiated the marriages at the toll houses.

From the south, those willing to sail might go to Southampton, Hampshire and purchase passage to the Channel Islands. The Isle of Guernsey in particular provided another alternative for a quick marriage. Of course, in the midst of the Napoleonic wars, sailing wasn't always a good option.

Closer to Home

A far less romantic but simpler, cheaper and closer to home alternative existed. All a couple really had to do was have their banns read for three consecutive weeks in a church, then have the ceremony performed.

In a large urban center, like London, parishes could be huge and the clergy hard-pressed to verify each couple's age and residency. If a couple could manage to get to a large town, or better London itself, they could lose themselves in the crowd and get married the conventional way. Their families were unlikely to get word of it in time to prevent anything.

That meant setting up residency, for at least a few weeks in the new city, likely 'living together in sin' as it were. A couple would have to manage room and board costs, but compared to travel expenses to Scotland, it could be far more reasonable. Naturally, a girl's reputation would be ruined in doing so, but if she was already bent on eloping, it probably didn't matter all that much to her.

After such a wedding occurred, the only recourse an aggrieved parent had was to go to the church where the banns had been called. There the parent, typically the father, would challenge that the banns had been mistaken or even fraudulent. The process was public, inconvenient and embarrassing. Worse still, even if the challenge was successful, the girl's reputation would likely be ruined and she would probably never marry well. So, challenges were not very common.

Despite a Gretna Green (or other Scottish) elopement being a romantic idyll, marrying in a big city parish was by far the most likely way young people married against their parents' wishes.

CHAPTER 11

Short, Simple and to the Point: Regency Weddings

Though nearly all of Jane Austen's works end with a wedding, she does not spend much time detailing the weddings themselves.

The bride was elegantly dressed; the two brides-maids were duly inferior; her father gave her away; her mother stood with salts in her hand, expecting to be agitated; her aunt tried to cry; and the service was impressively read by Dr Grant.~Mansfield Park

(Emma Woodhouse's wedding was) *"...very much like other weddings, where the parties have no taste for finery or parade and Mrs. Elton from the particulars detailed by her husband thought it all extremely shabby, and very inferior to her own. 'Very little white satin, very few lace veils; a most pitiful business!'" ~ Emma*

Today's brides may spend a year or more planning a wedding. Having a dress made, planning the reception in every detail and the cake—oh the cake!—are the stuff of many a young woman's dreams. So much so, discovering the details of a Regency era wedding might turn out a bit disappointing since most of the elaborate traditions we associate with weddings today originated decades later, during the Victorian Era

Wedding Dress

Modern brides often spend a great deal of effort and money on the wedding dress and expect to wear it only once. Honestly, it is hard to imagine another event where wearing one's wedding dress might be appropriate. Not exactly the sort of thing you'd wear to dinner, right?

In the regency era, though, the cost of textiles was so prohibitive that only royals like Princess Charlotte and equally wealthy brides even considered dresses that might only be worn once. A bride, like Charlotte Lucas of *Pride and Prejudice* or Harriet Smith of *Emma*, wore her 'best dress' for her wedding. A bride with some means, like Emma or even perhaps the Bennets, might have a new 'best dress' made for the occasion.

What might this 'best dress' look like? Unless one were quite wealthy, it would not be white. White garments required a huge amount of upkeep in an era where all wash was done by hand, so only the wealthiest wore it. Colored gowns were typical, with yellow, blue, pink and green being popular for several regency era years. Middle and lower class brides often chose black, dark brown and burgundy as practical colors that would wear well for years to come.

What did those gowns look like?

The gowns followed the fashionable trends of formal gowns of the day, but were largely indistinguishable from other formal gowns. *Ackerman's* and *La Belle Assemblee* fashion plates illustrate white gowns used for weddings. That was more indicative of the white gown being the most stylish of the era, rather than white being the wedding color. To set a bridal dress apart, finer materials and richer trims might be utilized if the bride could afford them: silks, satins and lace. The trims might be altered for wear after the wedding.

One major accessory that was missing: bridal veils. That fashion, though common in France, would not take hold in England until the Victorian era. Caps, hats, bonnets or flowers in the hair were common though.

"Since wedding gowns were often worn - to the point of being worn out - after the wedding, brides had to cherish something else. Often this was one of her wedding shoes, a natural choice given the lucky connotations of shoes in this context. Many carefully preserved satin slippers remain with notes inscribed in the instep attesting to the wearer's wedding." (Reeves-Brown, 2004)

GROOM'S ATTIRE

Men's formal attire was fairly well established, largely due to the influence of Beau Brummell: White shirts of muslin or linen; a white cravat, ideally in silk; a black or dark cut away, tailed jacket. Some period sources note grooms in light colored suits as well.

Coat buttons were left open to show a waistcoat. The waistcoat might be brightly colored and richly embroidered, the one place on a man's ensemble where bright colors were widely acceptable. Dark or black knee breeches, skin tight of course! Loose fitting trousers were generally not acceptable for a formal occasion until the later part of the regency. Black stockings and black pumps, never boots, and a top hat would finish the ensemble. Grooms of lesser means would wear the best garments they had.

Invitations and Announcements

Unlike weddings today, the wedding ceremony was not a widely attended event. Obviously the bride and groom, along with their witnesses, usually the bridesmaid and groomsman and the clergyman were there. Close family might be there and possibly local close friends, but that was all.

People did not generally travel to attend a wedding, so few if any invitations were issued. Neighbors and other well-wishers would not attend the service, but might wait outside the church for the newly married couple to emerge.

A newspaper announcement, in both national and local newspapers was, arguably, the most socially important aspect of the wedding. "Jane Austen once wrote, 'The latter writes me word that Miss Blackford is married, but I have never seen it in the papers, and one may as well be single if the wedding is not to be in print.'" (Forsling, 2011)

Mrs. Bennet of *Pride and Prejudice* complains,

> *"I suppose you have heard of it; indeed, you must have seen it in the papers. It was in the Times and the Courier, I know; though it was not put in as it ought to be. It was only said, 'Lately, George Wickham Esq., to Miss Lydia Bennet,' without there being a*

syllable said of her father, or the place where she lived, or anything. It was my brother Gardiner's drawing up too, and I wonder how he came to make such an awkward business of it. Did you see it?"

Things could have been much worse than Mrs. Bennet complained, though. Sometimes the announcements did not even give the name of the bride, just her father's name—and any titled connections, because who would dare forget them?

Ceremony

The bride named the day of the wedding, probably the only part of the prenuptial arrangements that was entirely under her control. Somehow, it seems in keeping with the attitude of the times, that what she had control over was effectively the least significant part of the process.

Remember, as early as the fifteenth century, English ecclesiastical courts equated a promise to marry with a legal marriage, so the ceremony was, for many, secondary to the betrothal.

Regency era wedding ceremonies were simple and entirely determined by the prescribed service in the Book of Common Prayer.Couples did not write their own vows or alter the service from what had been already established.

All weddings, except those by special license, took place between 8 AM and noon. Why? Honorable people had nothing to fear in the light of day and people would be more serious in the morning. Obvious, right?

Any day of the week was acceptable, though Sundays might be a bit inconvenient. Certain holy days, especially Lent were traditionally avoided.

Most people walked to church instead of riding in a carriage. Of course, most people did not have a carriage to ride in either. Flowers, herbs or rushes might be scattered on the route or at the church porch.

As with many weddings today, the bride's father (if present) would present the bride to the groom. The vows would be read from the Book of Common Prayer and a wedding ring, or rings exchanged.

Interestingly, a ring or rings were integral to the ceremony and it could not take place without them. The rings could be plain or ornate, precious metals like gold, or less dear materials like brass. "Lord Byron claimed that the wedding ring was 'the damnedest part of matrimony' but married men wore them as often as not, engraved with the couple's initials and the date of union." (Jones, 2009)

MARRIAGE LINES

After the ceremony, the clergyman, parish clerk, bride, groom, and two witnesses would proceed to the vestry to enter the 'marriage lines' into the parish register book. These 'lines' were explicitly set out in the Hardwicke Act and constituted the official record of the wedding, legal proof that it had taken place.

A copy of the records would be made and signed by all participants in the ceremony. The marriage lines would then be given to the new bride, notably her property, not the groom's.

Why?

Proof of her married state was much more important to a woman than to a man. Particularly among ... the lower classes, a woman's social standing, in some cases her very survival, depended upon her ability to prove she was a respectable married woman.

... A woman who was thought to be living with a man without benefit of clergy could be exposed to any number of dangers.

She could not depend on her husband for support if she could not prove she was his legal wife, ... she might even be liable to arrest and incarceration as a prostitute. If she was a widow, she could be denied her lawful dower rights, even custody of her own chil-

dren. ... her 'marriage lines' were proof of one of the most important achievements of her life, and might be her best protection against life's vicissitudes. (Kane, 2008)

Wedding Breakfast

Since weddings were held in the morning, the meal eaten afterwards was considered breakfast. "The breakfast was such as best breakfasts then were: some variety of bread, hot rolls, buttered toast, tongue or ham and eggs. The addition of chocolate [drinking chocolate] at one end of the table, and wedding cake in the middle, marked the specialty of the day." (Austen -Leigh, 1920)

Unlike the wedding ceremony, friends and relatives were usually invited to the wedding breakfast. Sometimes, though, as in the case of Charlotte Lucas of *Pride and Prejudice*, the bride and groom set off for the post-nuptial travels immediately from the church door, leaving their loved ones to celebrate on their own without them.

WEDDING CAKE

Though wedding cakes were baked for most weddings, they were very different from what we envision today. The cake resembled fruitcake, soaked with liberal amounts of alcohol: wine, brandy or rum. Usually the cakes would be covered in almond icing which was then browned in the oven. If a family wanted to display wealth, the cake would be covered in refined sugar icing and left very white. Pure white, refined sugar was very expensive and a sign of affluence. Elizabeth Raffald, in The Experienced English Housekeeper, published the first recipe for such an iced cake.

With all the alcohol, wedding cakes kept for a long time. Pieces would be sent home with family and friends, delivered to neighbors and even sent over distances to those who could not be part of the celebrations.

Honeymoons

After the wedding and possibly the breakfast, a newlywed couple would usually go to the husband's home. If the couple planned a wedding trip, they usually departed a week or so later.

Since the war (and finances for most people) made touring the continent out of the question, couples of the era usually planned trips closer to home. They might visit relations to make introductions (and cut down on travel costs) or visit picturesque landscapes like the Lake District or Peaks or seaside resorts like Brighton.

Often, the bride's sister or closest female friend accompanied the couple, as Julia did Maria in *Mansfield Park*. To the modern eye the custom seems weird at best, but since the bride and groom might have spent little time alone with one another prior to the wedding, relying only on one another for conversation and company could be very awkward. Having another person along could ease the transition for everyone.

Starting Married Life: Bridal Visits

When a couple arrived home, important social obligations in the form of social calls would begin. Typically, neighbors would call upon the new bride, often having first received one of her nuptial cards. These cards provided information including her new name, address, when the couple would be on their bridal travels, and the days she would be available to receive callers.

A bride could expect a month or more of exchanging visits and attending dinners and events in her honor as she became acquainted with her new community and learned her place in it. In *Emma*, the new Mrs. Elton takes the place of honor at the village ball and assumes it has been held in her honor because during the first months of marriage, a new bride was given the highest place at many social events.

CHAPTER 12

After the Wedding Comes a Marriage

All of Jane Austen's works involve the issues of finding the appropriate marriage partner and getting married in an era of changing expectations. Caught between the romanticism of the Victorian era and the rather sterile business arrangements of the early Georgian era, what did a typical regency era couple expect upon marriage?

The *Book of Common Prayer* (1662) made clear why (and why not) a couple should marry:

> *(Marriage) is not by any to be enterprised, nor taken in hand, unadvisedly, lightly, or wantonly, to satisfy men's carnal lusts and appetites, like brute beasts that have no understanding; but reverently, discreetly, advisedly, soberly, and in the fear of God;*

duly considering the causes for which Matrimony was ordained.

First, It was ordained for the procreation of children, to be brought up in the fear and nurture of the Lord, and to the praise of his holy Name.

Secondly, It was ordained for a remedy against sin, and to avoid fornication; that such persons as have not the gift of continency might marry, and keep themselves undefiled members of Christ's body.

Thirdly, It was ordained for the mutual society, help, and comfort, that the one ought to have of the other, both in prosperity and adversity.

However, nothing so intimately connected with the human heart could ever be so simple.

Age at marriage

Very wealthy men who did not need to establish themselves in the world might marry much younger women as Col. Brandon and Marianne Dashwood of *Sense and Sensibility* or Mr. Knightley and Emma of *Emma* did. At sixteen, Lydia Bennet of *Pride and Prejudice* would have been considered very young for marriage.

In general, middle class men and women married later than we might expect. Men usually delayed marriage until they were in a position to fully support a family. Sources put the average age of marriage between 23 and 27 for women and between 25 and 29 for men.

Postponing marriage had unintended consequences. It reduced the overall birthrate and typical family size. Perhaps coincidentally, or perhaps as a result of this, "the early nineteenth century also saw a rising proportion of marriages between London businessmen and the daughters of the gentry. From 1780 to 1820, as many ancient families died out in the male lineage, an increasingly large number of heiresses appeared on the marriage market."(Rendell, 2002)

The Institution of Marriage

For both men and women, marriage marked a transition into a new life. For men, it was a transition into full adulthood and an expectation of domestic comfort. (Vickery, 2009) In *Pride and Prejudice* Mr. Collins notes how he expects marriage will "add very greatly to my happiness" although his future wife, Charlotte Lucas believes that happiness in marriage is merely a matter of chance, not something she necessarily expected. Furthermore, marriage gave men the status of householder and a political voice in the community.

In general, beyond the ideal of a good dowry, men were looking for wives to bear them heirs, manage their households and be good companions. Marriage, though, was also viewed as a potential trap for the man. He would allow the woman to share in his money and social position and had no guarantee of receiving comparable benefits in return. (Shapard, 2003)

Conduct writers clearly expressed this sentiment. "Her Marriage is an Adoption into his Family, and therefore she is, to every Branch of it, to pay what their Stations there do respectively require." (*The Whole Duty of a Woman*, 1737)

Given a woman's legal coverture meant that she gave up her legal personhood in marriage, the attitude seems a bit ironic since she became the veritable possession of her husband.

In spite of limiting her legal rights, marriage immediately raised a woman's social status, no matter what her class. A married woman always took precedence over unmarried women. Lydia Bennet of *Pride and Prejudice* reminded her sisters of this when she returned from her marriage and insisted her sisters must 'go lower' because she was a married woman.

Who's in Charge Here?

Companionate marriages were desirable, but practical considerations were probably the backbone of most matches. Loving relationships were more likely to form after marriage than before, if they formed at all. Whatever amiable feelings might develop did so in the context of a clear hierarchy. In regency society, no one doubted that the husband was the head of the relationship, in charge of essentially everything

> *There cannot, indeed, be a sight more uncouth, than that of a man and his wife struggling for power: for where it ought to be vested, nature, reason, and Scripture, concur to declare;*
>
> *... How preposterous is it to hear a woman say, ' It shall be done!' —' I will have it so!' and often extending her authority not only beyond her jurisdiction, but in matters where he alone is competent to act, or even to judge. (Taylor, 1822)*

Under legal coverture, women had no legal existence; the husband existed for them both in public life. He owned all property, had custody of the children, conducted all business transactions on the family's behalf, even owned the wife's earnings should she have income of her own.

He even had the right to physically chastise

his wife, divide her from friends and family and severely curtail her movements, if he so wished. (Jones,2009) Mr. Darcy, could have legally forbidden Elizabeth from associating with her disgraceful relations had he chosen to do so.

Though this might sound like a recipe for creating petty tyrants, Rev. Thomas Gisborne (1797), a moralist of the era, argued that true marital harmony came from the husband taking pre-eminence over his wife. She need not fear though, if he were a religious man, he would follow God's will and be a kind protector for whom she would, in gratitude, be endlessly good tempered and pleasing. Sounds exactly like the marriage the Bennets of *Pride and Prejudice* enjoyed, doesn't it?

Maybe not so much.

While some may have strictly adhered to this view of marriage, most probably took a slightly softer stance more in keeping with the views of the Enlightenment. A growing respect for individuals meant that husbands were encouraged to see their wives as worthy human beings and respect their opinions. Marriages were probably not ones of equal give and take, but some degree of mutuality likely typified most relationships.

The unconventional Mrs. Croft from *Persuasion* argued this point with her brother, Capt. Wentworth, over dinner at the

Musgroves. She insists that women are rational creatures who do not expect to 'be in smooth water; all their days. After this conversation, Wentworth seems to grow in his regard for Anne Elliot as a competent, trustworthy helpmate during the course of the novel, perhaps transforming his perspective of the wifely role.

In general though, conduct writers agreed, it was right and appropriate for women to have the subservient role. Catherine Macaulay, a staunch promoter of female education held that husbands had the right to expect obedience from their wives, but that they should in their turn treat wives as their best friends. (Jones, 2009) Ann Taylor (1822) advocated, "A man of common understanding, though he may derive benefit from his wife's advice, certainly ought not to be governed by her."

Consequently, women needed to be prepared to be tolerant of a difficult husband. It was the price of being a married woman.

On your part, you promised to love as well as to honour and obey; and probably from the all-perfect being to whom you then surrendered yourself... But, however discreet your choice ... by degrees the discovery ... that you have married a mortal, and that the object of your affection is not entirely free from the infirmities of human nature. Then ... your disappointment may be moderated; and your love, so far from declining, may acquire additional tenderness, from the consciousness that there is room for mutual forbearance. (Taylor, 1822)

A proper wife had limited power for direct control over anything in her life, especially her husband. According to Gisborne (1797) her indirect influence should be channeled through affection, example and charms rather than through boldness or strength, all while being submitted to her husband's wishes in all things.

If all this seems a bit unfair, take heart, even conduct writers realized it: "The World in this is somewhat unequal, and the masculine Sex seems to play the Tyrant... "(*The Whole Duty of a Woman,* 1737) But fear not, there was compensation for the woman. "But if in this it lies under any Disadvantage, it is more than recompens'd, by having the Honour of Families in their Keeping. "(*The Whole Duty of a Woman,* 1737)

That certainly rectified all the disadvantages, right?

MUTUAL AFFECTION

Despite all the emphasis on male dominance and female subservience in marriage, marriages of affection were probably common. Among the lower class where spouses were most likely to be the same age, affection could blossom as women's joint participation in breadwinning placed them in partnership with their husbands. (Shoemaker, 1998)

Examining diaries and other personal documents of the period suggests that middle and upper class marriages were also often warm and affectionate, even on occasion blossoming into love. Shared values and goals between the partners could and did facilitate the development of warm friendships between spouses.

Ann Taylor's(1822) advice might also help: "A wife is tenderly alive to the kind attentions of her husband, whether at home or abroad: and neither can more gracefully fulfil the marriage vow, than by thus giving honour, open and cheerful honour, to whom honour is due."

If diaries and letters are to be believed though, passion played little role in these relationships. That may feel sad and hollow to the contemporary reader, but it is important to realize that individuals did not have the expectation of romance and passion in their marriages either. So, not having passion was not necessarily the disappointing blow that it would seem to the modern marriage seeker.

SPHERES OF FEMALE INFLUENCE

Regardless of the nature of her relationship with her husband, once a woman married, her focus was supposed to turn to entirely domestic pursuits.

> *The tour of a woman's gaiety should terminate with marriage. From that moment her pursuits should be solid, and her pleasures circumscribed within the limits of her household. ...The angel of courtship has sunk into a woman, and that woman will be valued principally as her fondness lies in retirement, and her pleasures near the nursery of her children. Nor are these pleasures small. Whatever fashion thinks, they have a secret relish, which the world cannot give.* (Bennett, 1811)

A woman was supposed to give herself entirely to managing her husband's domestic affairs, in both town and country if his wealth allowed for two houses. This included managing and educating children, handling budgets, clothing the entire family appropriately, feeding said family, managing all household chores herself or directing the staff who would accomplish them, handling social correspondence, entertaining and being a social asset to her husband in all ways.

Whew! A little exhausting just thinking about it.

Of course, even in this she could not just assume authority, but must act in accordance with her husband's wishes, even though conduct writers advised:

> *It is allowed, that every man should be master of his own house, a prerogative which he may preserve inviolate, without in the least interfering with that of his wife; and, in general, it will contribute more to his comfort if she is left to the quiet direction of those concerns which are more immediately within her province.* (Taylor, 1822)

All this does suggest that Jane Austen's heroines looked different to readers in her era than they do today. The Bennets' desire to marry for love is romantic to us, but would have seemed impractical and perhaps a little far-fetched in the era. Anne Elliot's initial refusal of Wentworth when he had little means of providing for a family was entirely rational, though sad, not a romantic tragedy. Emma Woodhouse's declaration that a spinster with money was respectable was not a statement of independence, but unrealistic conceit. The traits the modern reader is likely to celebrate were more demonstrations of imprudence for the Austen's original readers.

CHAPTER 13

Not Always a Happy Ending

Jane Austen only deals with the end of one marriage, the Rushworths', in *Mansfield Park*. Otherwise, her characters affirm the attitudes of regency society. Marriage was a nearly inviolable commitment, ending only with the death of a spouse.

"Ay, you may abuse me as you please," said the good-natured old lady; *"you have taken Charlotte off my hands, and cannot give her back again. So there I have the whip hand of you."* ~Mrs. Jennings to her son-in-law, *Sense and Sensibility*

"People that marry can never part, but must go and keep house together." ~ Catherine Morland defines matrimony, *Northanger Abbey*

Although, marriage in the regency era was regarded as a lifetime commitment, annulments, separations, and divorces were possible. However these remedies were difficult—in the case of the latter, nearly impossible—and unlike what modern readers know by those terms.

Annulment

Annulment, when possible, was the best option to end a marriage since it did not carry the social stigma of a divorce. An annulment voided a marriage making it as if it had never happened. Of course, that meant that if there any children, they were declared illegitimate since their parents had effectively never been married.

Annulment suits took place in an ecclesiastical court, presided upon by the bishop of the see containing the couple's parish. In general, the bishops were biased toward keeping marriages together, so they were unlikely to grant annulments for small technicalities like misspellings. They reserved the alternative for real issues.

What constituted a 'real issue'?

REASONS TO INVALIDATE A MARRIAGE

Violations of the Hardwicke Marriage Act were grounds to void a marriage. So if a couple was within the prohibited degrees of consanguinity, a marriage could be voided. The most likely scenario for this was when a man married his deceased wife's sister.

Bigamy would also void a marriage. If a person was already married to another, the first marriage held and the second was voided.

In addition, a marriage was considered voidable under conditions of fraud, incompetence or impotence.

FRAUD

Fraud could take two forms.

If the wedding license or the banns contained fictitious names, an annulment might be granted. Since the purpose of the banns was to allow people to speak out if they knew a problem that would prevent a wedding, correct names were essential. Names used had to be the participant's name or a name that they had been widely known by. Inadvertent mistakes and spelling errors didn't count. In those cases, the bishop would correct the official records and disallow the annulment.

A far less common form of fraud occurred when one party could not fulfil promises they made in the marriage contract. So, if the groom did not have property he claimed to have —as might have happened when Edward Ferrars lost his inheritance in *Sense and Sensibility*— or a father could not deliver on a promised dowry—as might be the case of someone like Anne Elliot of *Persuasion*— breach of contract could be claimed and a marriage voided.

Forced marriage, where one or the other was coerced and did not give willing consent to the marriage, would also constitute fraud.

INCOMPETENCE

Legal incompetence of either party rendered a marriage voidable. This could come in two forms.

If one were underage to enter into a legal contract, they were considered incompetent in the eyes of the law. So if an underage person did not have a guardian's permission to marry, the marriage might be annulled.

In reality though, a father rarely would insist that a wayward daughter's marriage be annulled. Such an act would ruin her reputation and it would be difficult or impossible to see her married off thereafter. Thus, sixteen-year-old Lydia Bennet of *Pride and Prejudice* could be reasonably certain her father would not insist her marriage to Wickham be annulled.

Insanity would also render one legally incompetent. But being proved insane, generally meant a person would be locked away for the rest of their lives, with all their possessions under the control of a guardian. Even worse, it tainted the entire family. Think of Mrs. Rochester in Jane Eyre. The wife of a man declared insane would be considered ruined. So this was not an attractive option for a family who disapproved of a marriage.

IMPOTENCE

If insanity was not an attractive option for gaining an annulment, then impotence was even worse.

Proving impotence meant a man must (faithfully) share a bed with his wife for three years and prove she was still a virgin. The mind boggles at how this might be accomplished to satisfy a court. Then with the help of a couple of court appointed courtesans, he must prove he cannot achieve an erection. Seriously. Then he might be declared impotent—and utterly humiliated.

WHAT ABOUT NON-CONSUMMATION?

Though a convenient plot device for romance writers, non-consummation of marriage was not considered a reason for annulment. Only the possibility of consummation was required.

Since annulments were so limited, most unhappy couples could not seek one. Their only options were to learn to live with each other or to pursue divorce.

Divorce

Until the last few years of the seventeenth century England was a land without divorce. After that, divorce was possible, but very, very difficult. "Between 1670 and 1857, 379 Parliamentary divorces were requested and 324 were granted. Of those 379 requests, eight were by wives, and only four of those were granted." (Wright, 2004)

Before the Matrimonial Causes Act of 1857, which finally legalized divorce in the civil courts, divorce was governed by the ecclesiastical court and the canon law of the Church of England.

The Church of England opposed ending a marriage. It only allowed a couple a 'divorce' that amounted to what we today call a legal separation. Parties could break up housekeeping and were no longer legally and financially responsible for one another. But, and this is the big one, they could not remarry. It was also an expensive process, out of the reach of most, but far more affordable than a parliamentary divorce.

To obtain a divorce in the sense of what we understand today, the dissolution of a marriage allowing the parties to remarry other people, Parliament had to step in and declare the couple an exception to the law of the land. Hence divorce truly required an act of Parliament.

The process could take two years and involve three separate trials. The first would be obtaining a 'divorce' (legal separation) from one of the Consistory Courts. Then a criminal conviction proving adultery (criminal conversation) would be necessary. Finally, a Private Act of Divorcement would be brought before Parliament. If granted, the marriage was dissolved and one or both parties could remarry.

LEGAL SEPARATION

Canon law allowed an action called the divortium a mensa et thoro (separation from bed and board). The Ecclesiastical courts permitted it only for a very limited set of causes: life-threatening cruelty and adultery by the husband, or adultery by the wife. This act allowed spouses to live separately and ended the woman's coverture to her husband and his financial responsibility for her.

Similar private arrangements might be made that didn't involve the courts or require accusations of misbehavior toward either party. These agreements spelled out terms for maintenance, economic freedom and often even included clauses preventing the husband from disturbing his ex-wife.

Unfortunately, these were legally dubious and often didn't hold up in court. Technically a woman was still under coverture no matter what the agreement might say.

If a spouse, man or wife, simply ran off and deserted the other, the doctrine of coverture complicated matters, because they were still legally one person. A woman could not simply leave her husband's home without permission. He could legally drag her back under his roof—and even soundly beat her for her efforts!

If she managed to leave, she had no access to moneys or properties from the marriage, everything belonged to the husband. Nor did she have any right to her children. They too belonged to their father—assuming of course he wanted them.

The only part of coverture that did not favor the man in this situation was that he remained liable for his wife's debts whether she was in his house or not. So, if she could manage to get credit, her husband would be liable.

Neither a separation from bed and board nor an informal separation agreement actually ended the marriage. According to civil law, the marriage still existed.

REASONS FOR DIVORCE

In order for remarriage to be a possibility, the marriage had to either be annulled or a divorce granted. If divorce were pursued, there were several acceptable causes for divorce. Adultery was by far the most common. This was already a requirement for the church to grant a separation, but no matter, it all had to be proved again in civil court.

All adultery was not created equal. Adultery

by the wife was considered sufficient grounds for a husband to obtain divorce. For the wife, adultery had to be aggravated by physical cruelty (if he beat her to the point of threatening her life), bigamy (which no one thought was a good idea) or incest (like sleeping with the woman's sister, clearly a capital notion for marital harmony, right?)

CRIMINAL CONVERSATION

Since a man's wife was one legal person with her husband, he could not bring a criminal complaint against her for adultery. To complicate matters further, it was not against the law to sleep with another man's wife, so aggrieved husbands had to get a little creative in dealing with the problem.

Civil laws concerning trespassing were used in bringing a wife's lover to court since he ostensibly 'wounded another man's property'. Given a wife was by law, effectively chattel, a husband suffered damage to her chastity when adultery occurred, thus entitling him to financial compensation under civil law. If she ran off with her lover, the husband could also claim damages for the loss of her services as household manager, arguably one of her more valuable contributions to her husband's household.

The euphemistic name for the offense was 'Criminal Conversation' (crim con.)

If a husband had evidence of adultery, he could launch a civil crim con case against the other man. Thus, he might vindicate his own honor and destroy his rival's character and finances, all without the unsavory shedding of blood in a duel.

Interestingly, the wife was not a party in a crim con suit, only her alleged lover. What's more, women were not permitted to bring suit against other women for adultery with their husbands. (Remember the whole coverture thing? That.)

Criminal Conversation Trials

The last decade of the 18th century was the heyday for the crim con trial. Lord Chief Justice Lloyd Kenyon declared that the country was in the grip of a "crisis of morality." (Fullerton, 2004) Only after the average award settlements dropped in the early 19th century did the number of claims begin to decline. Wonder if there's a connection...

In any case, crim con trials tended to be colorful, highly publicized events at the Court of the King's Bench, in a corner of Westminster Hall. These trials were open to the general public, as close to modern reality TV as the regency era could get. And for those not fortunate enough to be able to attend in person, most book sellers carried newspapers, pamphlets, transcripts and 'true' exposés documenting all the sexual misadventures of high society.

Barristers on both sides of the case played up the drama as much for the public notoriety as for the effect on the court's decisions. They called servants, especially young pretty ones, to deliver testimony for both the plaintiff and the defense. While servants could be (mostly) excused for presenting salacious tales in coarse language, the barristers were gentlemen and adopted notably euphemistic and flowery language to express the necessary elements with decency and taste. Some said it became something of an art form.

With so much at stake, both in terms of finances and reputations, truth and accuracy fell to the need to convince jurors.

> *The defendant, if he could not deny that he had seduced the plaintiff's wife, was obliged to present the object of his attentions as a low, debauched, corrupted woman who was worthless to the world let alone her sorry husband. The plaintiff, in order to secure a high payout, had to present his marriage as an unending festival of joyous love and his unfaithful wife as the best and most innocent woman in the world before the wicked seducer got his grubby hands on her.* (Wilson, 2007)

As a rule, these trials progressed quickly

and once damages were assessed, they were enforceable like any other debt.

Damage Awards

In deciding damages, the jury had several factors to consider. The rank and fortune of the parties helped determine the loss the husband had suffered, effectively setting a cash value of the wife before her seduction. Juries also weighed the length of the marriage and the affair, whether the two men were friends before the seduction, and whether or not said seduction had taken place in the marital bed (an even greater outrage and offense.) In many cases, juries were motivated to see a well-heeled rake was sufficiently punished to deter more of his kind from following in his footsteps.

Juries often awarded only half the damages requested, so indignant gentlemen just increased the amount they asked for, often sums totaling over £15,000. Occasional cases were settled for up to £20,000 but awards of at least £1,500 were far more common.

SPOUSAL ABUSE

A husband's adultery was not thought to be as much of an injury as a wife's since any children in the marriage were assumed to be the husband's. His property and money would be spent on their upkeep and eventually be their inheritance. Clearly, he had much more to lose in the matter than she did. So in a divorce proceeding, a woman had to prove both adultery and cruelty.

If she could not prove bigamy or that her husband was sleeping with a close relation, a woman was in the unfortunate position of having to prove him intolerably cruel.

Not surprisingly, a woman's legal coverture made this difficult.

According to Blackstone (1765)

The husband also, by the old law, might give his wife moderate correction. For, as he is to answer for her misbehaviour, the law thought it reasonable to intrust him with this power of restraining her, by domestic chastisement, in the same moderation that a man is allowed to correct his apprentices or children; for whom the master or parent is also liable in some cases to answer.

But this power of correction was confined within reasonable bounds, and the husband was prohibited from using any violence to his wife, aliter quam ad virum, ex causa regiminis et castigationis uxoris suae, licite et rationabiliter pertinet.[Otherwise than lawfully and reasonably belongs to the husband for the due government and correction of his wife.] The civil law gave the husband the same, or a larger, authority over his wife: allowing him, for some misdemeanors, flagellis et fustibus acriter verberare uxorem;[To beat his wife severely with scourges and sticks.] for others, only modicam castigationem adhibere. [To use moderate chastisement] (Translations from Latin, Jones, 1905)

In short, a man had the right to severely beat his wife if he deemed it appropriate. This made proving cruelty very difficult.

So much for Blackstone's (1765) assertion: "so great a favourite is the female sex of the laws of England."

It is comforting to remember that Judge Buller amended this understanding somewhat, with his 'rule of thumb': A man could thrash his wife with a stick no thicker than his thumb.

Ironically, instead of improving women's lot, the ideals of companionate marriage may have made domestic violence worse. The incompatible expectations of men raised in a patriarchal tradition, legal coverture, and the social enlightenment were ripe to create tensions that could easily explode into violence.

A woman could petition the court that her husband inflicted cruel and unjust harm upon her. She could charge her husband with assault and battery or could 'swear the peace' by which a court could order her husband to keep the peace if he had inflicted physical injury, imprisonment or some other cruelty on her. (Laudermilk,1989) But to get the sympathy of the court, women had to paint themselves as passive and dutiful victims of truly inhumane treatment. It could be done, but it was difficult at best as evidenced in that of the three hundred twenty four divorces granted between 1670 and 1857, only four were granted to women. (Wright, 2004)

PARLIAMENTARY DIVORCE

After receiving a legal separation from an adulterous wife and seeing her declared guilty in a crim con trial, a man could go his separate way, repaid for the damages of his wife's infidelity. Only a few could afford (or were willing to take) the final step that would allow them to remarry as they chose, a parliamentary divorce.

Cost was not the only deterrent to a parliamentary divorce. The proceedings were long, messy and very public. Few honorable men wanted their names and private business made part of the public press, to be enjoyed by the 'Great Unwashed'. Moreover, simply being involved in a divorce proceeding was enough to get one shunned by good society and banned from Royal Court. So only three or four cases a year made it before Parliament.

When a Private Act (or Bill) of Divorcement was brought before Parliament, the bill had three readings before the Lords. Witnesses to support the allegations of (almost always the wife's) adultery had to be present for the second reading. The wife though, could not testify in her own defense because at this point, she still has no legal personhood separate from her husband.

If a divorce was granted, it overturned the property settlements made in the marriage articles. Parliament took on the responsibility of redistributing assets. Typically, the woman (since in almost all cases, she was the guilty adulterer) lost all her income, property and any right to see her children.

Mr. Rushworth of *Mansfield Park* was legally entitled to keep Maria Bertram's dowry; her adultery meant she forfeited all rights to it. Usually a woman was granted an allowance to maintain herself, just enough for food and housing in most cases. But, since she was not permitted to sue her ex-husband, the chances of her actually collecting that allowance were slim.

Although one of the advantages of a parliamentary divorce was the ability to remarry, a divorced woman could not remarry unless the divorcement settlement specifically gave her permission to do so. Clauses could be included in the settlement that would explicitly forbid her from marrying the man with whom she had committed adultery.

Not entirely surprising, huh?

As Mary Crawford observed in *Mansfield Park*, polite society would not accept a divorced woman into their company. 'Good dinners and large parties' could only go so far in altering the prevailing attitude that a divorced woman should spend the rest of her life secluded and atoning for her effrontery. Even family members were apt to ostracize such a woman. In the very rare case that the woman was not considered the guilty party, she would still suffer censure in the eyes of society. Guilty or innocent, the ex-husband would also endure some social losses, but never as much as the woman.

CHAPTER 14

Widowhood

Jane Austen's works were populated with numerous widows, representing all walks of life. Austen presents her readers the poor and nearly destitute Mrs. Bates (*Emma*) and Mrs. Smith (*Persuasion*; the wealthy and titled: Lady Catherine (*Pride and Prejudice*), Lady Russell and the Dowager Lady Dalrymple (*Persuasion*); and widowers Mr. Woodhouse (*Emma*), Sir Walter Elliot (*Persuasion*), General Tilney (*Northanger Abbey*), and Admiral Crawford (*Mansfield Park*). Between the extremes we find Mrs. Clay (*Persuasion*), Mrs. Dashwood (*Sense and Sensibility*), and Mrs. Norris (*Mansfield Park*) and the notable Lady Susan (*Lady Susan*).

From the very poor to the very well off, death of a spouse was a common experience. High mortality broke up nearly as many marriages then as divorce does today. (Shoemaker,

1998) Many individuals were widowed in middle age.

Widowers

As in life, marriage did not affect men and women equally in death. It is no coincidence that Jane Austen's widowers were neither impoverished nor dependent upon the kindness of others for survival. Widowers rarely faced financial difficulties due solely to the loss of their spouse. The only Austen widower who faced financial hardships was Sir Walter Elliot of *Persuasion*. Ironically, his financial issues were caused by the loss of his wife's prudent household management.

Outside of problems like these, though, widowers experienced little financial change at the death of their wives. Due to coverture, the husband already owned everything that was not set aside in a separate estate. He retained a life interest (curtesy) in all his dead spouse's land, not just the one third specified by dower laws. (Curtesy is a common law principle in England and early America by which a widower could use property held in his deceased wife's name until his own death, but could not sell or transfer it to anyone but the children of his wife. (Lewis))

At his death and not before, the property would go to his wife's heirs. Unlike a husband's heirs who collected their inheritance immediately, a wife's heirs got no land until the husband died.

Mourning protocols for widowers did not include the extensive restrictions experienced by women. They were not expected to dress in mourning garb nor delay remarriage for at least a year. Widowers frequently remarried quickly, without societal censure, especially if he was left with young children.

Widows

When a woman's husband died, she was expected to spend a full year (long enough for a baby conceived in her marriage to be born) in full or deep mourning. During this time she was expected to dress in all black, refraining from public appearances. Movie adaptations of *Sense and Sensibility* portray Mrs. Dashwood in widow's weeds. The next six months she would wear subdued colors like greys and lavenders, suitable for half-mourning and begin a slow reintroduction into society.

Many conduct writers suggested a widow should continue to live a life of somber retirement for the remainder of her life. Without the man who defined her legal personhood, society had a difficult time understanding what to do with her. Keeping her out of sight and out of mind was one way of dealing with that.

Widowhood effected women differently, according to their stations in life and the arrangements at the time of her marriage. They might enjoy freedoms they never previously experienced, find themselves thrust into desperation and poverty, or something in between.

UPPER CLASS WIDOWS

A woman could become the mistress of her own destiny at the death of her husband. If her marriage had been blessed with property and assets, she might be fortunate enough to receive a dower or jointure that could support her in her widowhood.

Until the 1833 formal repeal of common law dower, a woman was entitled to a one third share in the real property her husband owned. The share could be increased in his will. (Lewis) This meant, though, that his estate could not be fully settled during his wife's lifetime. So, the 1833 law overturned dower in favor of jointures set up in the marriage articles. Though jointure provisions were often made in settlements prior to 1833, after that they were the only provision a widow could depend upon. (Davidoff, 1987)

Unlike a wife's estate, distributions from a husband's estate, as well as the repayment of debt, were due upon the man's death, not the death of his spouse. In most cases, the widow was not the heir to the estate. So widows of wealthy men, like Mrs. Dashwood in *Sense and Sensibility*, could find themselves homeless and with very little means. Norland, the Dashwood estate was inherited by the son of a first marriage who had no obligation to the current Mrs. Dashwood or her daughters. She and her daughters had to make do on the jointure derived from her dowry. Similarly, the Bennet women of *Pride and Prejudice* expected to lose their home when Mr. Bennet died and his heir Mr. Collins assumed the property.

Not all women suffered such unhappy fates. Some received substantial dowers or jointure arrangements, which allowed them to continue to live comfortably and independently. Both Lady Russell of *Persuasion* and Lady Catherine of *Pride and Prejudice* enjoyed this enviable state. Without coverture to limit them, they held and managed their own assets in ways married women could not. Many widows in these circumstances did not remarry as to do so would mean the loss of their assets and freedoms when they entered the coverture of their new husband.

Wives of peers also retained their titles after their husband's death. The title 'Dowager' might be added to her name, if the son who inherited his father's title were married. His wife would take the title (countess, duchess etc.) and his mother would become the Dowager countess, duchess, etc.

LOWER CLASS WIDOWS

Upper class, independent widows were by and large, rare creatures. Far more common were the widows for whom a husband's death sent them and their children into desperate states.

The loss of the primary breadwinner could send a family spiraling into dependency and poverty. By age 65, one third of widows depended on the state or charity. Many ended up in workhouses or other institutions. Society was often hostile or at least suspicious toward widows both because of the potential burden to society they represented and their uncertain social role lacking a man to legally define their personhood. (Shoemaker, 1998)

Mrs. Smith of *Persuasion* is such a woman. The collapse of her late husband's affairs and the refusal of his executor to make efforts to right them meant she was destitute. Her illness confined her to her meager rented rooms and she had no one to speak for her and compel the executor to act appropriately—until Wentworthstepped in. Without his help, she would doubtlessly have become one of those widows dependent upon charity.

Ironically, the widows of church vicars and curates often experienced such a plight. The church offered no provisions for clergy widows. So, like Mrs. Bates in *Emma* or Jane Austen's own mother, they were often reduced to dependency upon family and friends for their maintenance. Mrs. Norris from *Mansfield Park* might have enjoyed a jointure funded through her dowry, but her taking residence with Sir Thomas suggests she was economizing after her husband's death.

Lady Susan (of—wait for it—*Lady Susan*) provides another example. Though obviously upper class, her spending has reduced her circumstances and she no longer has a residence of her own. She flits from the home of one friend or relative to another, essentially living on their kindness. Since her behavior was putting an end to that resource, were it not for her marriage to Sir James Martin, she would likely have been in quite dire straits.

WIDOWS OF THE MIDDLING SORT

Widows of the middle class might find themselves possessed of the means to enter into public life and earn an income without resorting to prostitution.

Single women and widows were able to exercise the same property rights as men. In some parishes they were even permitted to vote. Interestingly, they were entered in the tax records as 'widows' instead of by their occupation as men were, presumably because men's occupations were far more important to defining them than were women's. (Shoemaker, 1998)

What occupations might a widow take on?

WIDOWS' OCCUPATIONS

The options a widow might have open to her varied widely with the resources available to her. Without education or assets she might seek a position as a housekeeper, either among relatives, or a paid position in a household.

If left with some education and some accomplishments, she might hire herself out as a governess or lady's companion. Mrs. Jenkinson and Mrs. Younge, companions to young ladies of *Pride and Prejudice* were both likely widows.

Others turned to writing books on a variety of subjects including: children, household and cookbooks, conduct books and also history, biography and science. Publishing for public recognition was considered unwomanly, so many women published anonymously.

"Although publishing on commission was considered perfectly respectable, female writers usually preferred to sell the copyright of their works ... She was paid by the publisher in a lump sum either on acceptance of the manuscript or within a year of publication of the book. No further com-

munication need take place between him and the author until the end of the 14 or 28 years for which the copyright had been purchased." (Collins, 1998)

If a woman had a house, she was in the happy position to be able to rent rooms to lodgers putting both her housekeeping expertise and her property to good use. A woman with some education and a house might use her home to run a school, possibly with the help of her older daughters.

With sufficient capital, a widow might continue on with her husband's business. While too much ambition, especially for a high income, was discouraged, she would be permitted to enter into the market place. Shops and even farms might be and often were headed by widows.

Widows left with capital but no business often invested in loans or property and lived off the proceeds. "Research suggests that widows owned a sizable proportion of the London housing stock and played a vital role in the provision of loan capital through the bond and mortgage markets." (Shoemaker, 1998) Female capital supported the joint stock companies behind municipal utilities and railways. Widows and spinsters were the core of those investors requiring a steady income without administrative worries. (Davidoff, 2002) Interesting, the important economic role played by individuals society didn't have a place for.

Remarriage

While men often remarried quickly after the death of their wives with nary an eyebrow raised, women faced varying degrees of opposition to remarrying. Custom decreed that they should spend a year in deep mourning for their husband, so a woman who married sooner than that was extremely suspect. Conduct manuals strongly urged widows to honor their husband's memories rather than go about looking for further married felicity. After all, one could not reasonably expect to be fortunate enough to find two good husbands in a single lifetime, right?

Soldiers' wives, especially those who 'followed the drum' and accompanied their husbands on deployment often remarried within days or even hours of their husband's demise. They were deeply criticized as hardened, unfeminine creatures.

The choice though was usually one of necessity. Not only would a widow lose her husband's income, but if she followed her husband on deployment and worked in the camp as she would be expected to do, she would lose both her privilege of working there and her way home without her husband.

Finding another husband was a matter of survival.

Society though, was more apt to consider the remarriage a consequence of voracious sexual appetite. The prevailing belief was that once a woman was introduced to sexual activity, she would be consumed by lust. This makes the character of Lady Susan a much more understandable choice; Austen was merely portraying the contemporary stereotype of a widow—a woman on the prowl to fulfill her baser motives.

Special condemnation was reserved for older widows interested in younger men. For when

> *...old Women marry young Men. Indeed, any Marriage is in such, a Folly and Dotage. They who must suddenly make their Beds in the Dust, what should they think of a Nuptial Couch... But this Dotage becomes perfect Frenzy and Madness when they choose young Husbands; This is an Accumulation of Absurdities and Contradictions. The Husband and the Wife are but one Person; and yet at once young and old, fresh and withered. It is reversing the Decrees of Nature.* (The Whole Duty of a Woman, 1737)

The only possible reason a man could want to marry an older widow would be for her money. Such fortune hunting, though, was generally frowned upon. A wealthy virgin though, she would be an entirely acceptable choice.

CHAPTER 15

Behind Closed Doors

Though Jane Austen did not write explicitly about sexual relations, she was no doubt aware of the goings-on between men and women. Both Maria Bertram (*Mansfield Park*) and Lady Susan (*Lady Susan*) suggest she was well versed in the licentiousness of her era.

Modern readers often view the regency era through the lens of Victorian writers, seeing it as a period of purity, restraint and virtue—as the Victorians wished it had been. However, the regency was anything but.

Debauchery and excess started at the top of the social order and trickled down through the ranks. It wasn't until after the Queen Caroline affair of 1820, when the wife of George IV was accused of adulterous relations, that public attitudes toward marriage and sexuality began to change. A "belief in the unblemished nature of English womanhood, an insistence that femininity meant virtue and honor" took hold and the beginning of Victorian morality formed. (Davidoff, 2002)

Sexual Morality

The Victorian view of sexuality, with the woman as passive and essentially desexualized was rooted in the use of the microscope. With it, scientists discovered that male sperm was 'active' and female ova were 'passive'. Thus they concluded that "female pleasure wasn't necessary for conception to occur. This realization in principle steadily eroded all notions about sexual equalism and the necessary legitimacy of pleasure-taking woman." (Gatrell, 2006)

Prior to that discovery, consistent with Greek philosophy, most people believed that "each sex harbored 'seeds' that must be simultaneously ejaculated if conception was to occur." (Gatrell, 2006) So not only were women capable of enjoying sex as much as men, it was actually rather important that they did. This notion flourished into the 1810s.

Ironically, many believed that women had very strong sexual drives and once awaked, they could become insatiable. At the end of the eighteenth century, articles in the fashionable Bon Ton Magazine took for granted that women were the more voracious and passionate sex; and visual satires and erotica implied this as well. (Gatrell, 2006)

Parents and guardians did not want to see this desire awakened before marriage lest it lead a young woman into prostitution. So premarital sex—sex before betrothal, remember it was all about the contract not the ceremony—was frowned upon.

PORNOGRAPHY

There is a widespread belief during the regency that young women were so sheltered that they went into marriage with little exposure to what went on between men and women behind closed doors. While in some cases that might have been true, it was not because sex was not presented openly in society.

Erotic imagery, often classified as satire, was easy to find in metropolitan areas. Print shops displayed explicit images of men and women both inside the shops and on the windows facing main streets where anyone could see them. The images depicted both men and women, in various states of undress, engaged in conventional and unconventional sex acts. (Shoemaker, 1998) Few would publicly defend obscene prints, but they were largely tolerated. (Wilson, 2007)

The prints themselves were expensive, out of the range of most people. So, most admirers had to enjoy them through the shop windows.

The upper class though, maintained a steady demand for the prints. King George IV was a collector. After his death, a considerable collection of 'erotic satires' was discovered and destroyed by his executor. (Shoemaker, 1998)

Sex and courting

Conduct manuals strongly urged young women to preserve their virtue until marriage. "The Civility of Women, which is always to be preserved, must not be carried to a Compliance, which may betray them into irrecoverable Mistakes." (*The Whole Duty of a Woman*, 1737).

This increased emphasis may, in part, have come from the Hardwicke Marriage Act. The act removed legal protections for the betrothed that forced men to marry if the woman became pregnant. (Shoemaker, 1998) However, given that about thirty percent of babies were born in the first seven months of marriage, it is clear that a great many did not abide by this advice. (Heydt-Stevenson, 2005)

Despite the supervision of chaperones, courtships did include elements of sexual encouragement, fondling and discovery. (Shoemaker, 1998) After an offer of marriage was made and accepted, supervision of the couple dropped dramatically. Since a man's honor was deeply valued—and breach of promise suits a strong possibility—once betrothed, one was essentially married.

Once married, a man held his wife's fate in his hands. He expected her full obedience. He could legally restrict her movement; deny her access to her family and friends; even beat her for misbehavior. So denying his advances during betrothal probably did not look like a good idea for long term felicity in marriage.

Sex in marriage

The ideal of an early nineteenth century marriage was one where the more mature husband would care for, guide and advise his young wife. Love , would be tender rather than passionately erotic. Those desires would likely be exercised with a mistress or courtesan. (Davidoff, 2002)

Many men felt after they had bestowed their name and fortune on a woman that they had done their part. Marriage was an institution for the begetting of heirs and creation of a household, not the proper place for passion. (Laudermilk, 1989)

Austen echoes these sentiments in her treatment of Charlotte Lucas and Mr. Collins in *Pride and Prejudice*. Their marriage reflects the sentiments of an earlier era when love, if it happened, occurred after marriage and sexual relations were part of the contract. Charlotte's contentment in marriage suggests that she does not struggle in sharing a bed with her husband. Perry (2000) writes:

> *One is surprised by Austen's acquittal of Charlotte ... In our day, the institution of marriage with a repellant man would be an insupportable form of prostitution. Yet Charlotte Lucas willingly undertakes all the offices of her new station, from visiting Lady Catherine de Bourgh several times a week to sleeping with Mr. Collins... There is not the slightest whiff of sexual disgust about the matter: ...the physical repugnance that we in the present century feel at the idea of sleeping with Mr. Collins , is entirely absent in Jane Austen's treatment of the matter. The "better feelings" that Charlotte Lucas is said to have sacrificed do not, apparently, include squeamishness about sex with a pompous and sycophantic man.*

Perry (2000) goes on to suggest that 'sexual disgust' at sharing a bed with a man one did not love was an invention of "the eighteenth century, one dimension of an evolving sexual identity for women that could control their sexual reactions without interference—whether political or protective—of a network of kin relations." But it did not fully permeate society until well into the nineteenth century with the emphasis on romantic love , in marriage. Thus, the activities of the marriage bed could be about mutual satisfaction-- remember most thought this necessary for conception—despite the marriage itself being more about companionability than love.

A brief aside: In her treatment of Elizabeth Bennet and Mr. Darcy, and her own refusal of Mr. Bigg-Wither's (a real life Mr. Collins) proposal of marriage, Austen demonstrates a more modern sensibility toward love and marriage. "Jane Austen, who must have liked him (Bigg-Wither) well enough humanly, was miserable when she envisioned being married to him, shows her elevated expectations of marriage. She was not attracted to Harris Bigg-Wither and could not, in the words of Wollstonecraft, violate 'the purity of her own feelings.'" (Perry, 2000)

Sex outside of Marriage

Some marriages were based on true affection, but it was often a friendly affection, not a passionate one. It was expected that spouses, men in particular, would seek pleasure outside marriage if it were not to be found within. Wives might be permitted discreet affairs, after a male child was born, but men were granted much wider license. (Gatrell, 2006)

MISTRESSES

Wealthy men often maintained both a wife

and a mistress. While the Church decried the behavior, nearly all the Royal Princes flaunted their mistresses and recognized their bastard children, even granting some titles. Gentlemen were often godfathers to their bastard sons and frequently helped them establish themselves in the world. Some literary analysts have suggested the elder Mr. Darcy's, treatment of Wickham in *Pride and Prejudice* implied that Wickham was the senior Darcy's illegitimate son.

Kept women would be established according to the wealth of their lover. Usually they were established in a household of their own. At the end of *Persuasion* Mrs. Clay is established in London under the protection of William Elliot. Installing one's mistress in one's home as the Crawford's uncle did in *Mansfield Park* was not appropriate—especially with a single woman like Mary Crawford in the household.

Men were regularly seen in public with their mistresses (though not in front of their wives, that would be disrespectful). Often they drew up contracts with their mistresses, explicitly laying out the financial terms of their arrangements. Unlike the wife, the mistress would be entitled to keep her money and use it as she wished. A man might pay a premium to have exclusive rights to his mistress, but it wasn't uncommon for such a woman to have discreet affairs on the side. Actresses and dancers were often sought after as mistresses.

VENEREAL DISEASE

Not only did a wife have to bear the weight of her husband's affairs with no power to stop them, she also ran the risk of contracting venereal disease from his wanderings. Estimates suggested that as much as 15% of the population of Paris and London had both syphilis and gonorrhea, but the proportion was higher among the elite circles. Doctors were known to treat ladies infected by their husbands without informing either party of the diagnosis. (Kelly, 2006)

Medical writers of the era believed women to be the source of infection. (Somehow that isn't surprising, is it?) Some suggested the secretions of an uninfected woman could produce a spontaneous case of syphilis in a man. Others believed that too much or too little sex, sex during menstruation or after too much alcohol could cause gonorrhea in men while leaving the woman unaffected. (Heydt-Stevenson, 2005)

Heat and mercury were the go-to cures for venereal disease. Gowland's lotion which contained mercury was a common prescription for syphilis. Since freckles were considered a sign of sexual disease, (Fullerton, 2004) it does make one wonder what Austen was implying when Sir Water Elliot of *Persuasion* noted Mrs. Clay's constant use of Gowland's lotion had carried away her freckles. Perhaps it was merely coincidental, but then again, perhaps not.

Form of Solemnization of Matrimony

From: The Book of Common Prayer, 1662

First the Banns of all that are to be married together must be published in the Church three several Sundays, during the time of Morning Service, or of Evening Service, (if there be no Morning Service,) immediately after the second Lesson; the Curate saying after the accustomed manner,

I PUBLISH the Banns of Marriage between M. of _____ and N. of _____. If any of you know cause, or just impediment, why these two persons should not be joined together in holy Matrimony, ye are to declare it. This is the first [second, or third] time of asking.

And if the persons that are to be married

dwell in divers Parishes, the Banns must be asked in both Parishes; and the Curate of the one Parish shall not solemnize Matrimony betwixt them, without a Certificate of the Banns being thrice asked, from the Curate of the other Parish.

At the day and time appointed for solemnization of Matrimony, the persons to be married shall come into the body of the Church with their friends and neighbours: and there standing together, the Man on the right hand, and the Woman on the left, the Priest shall say,

DEARLY beloved, we are gathered together here in the sight of God, and in the face of this congregation, to join together this Man and this Woman in holy Matrimony; which is an honourable estate, instituted of God in the time of man's innocency, signifying unto us the mystical union that is betwixt Christ and his Church; which holy estate Christ adorned and beautified with his presence, and first miracle that he wrought, in Cana of Galilee; and is commended of Saint Paul to be honourable among all men: and therefore is not by any to be enterprised, nor taken in hand, unadvisedly, lightly, or wantonly, to satisfy men's carnal lusts and appetites, like brute beasts that have no understanding; but reverently, discreetly, advisedly, soberly, and in the fear of God; duly considering the causes for which Matrimony was ordained.

First, It was ordained for the procreation of children, to be brought up in the fear and nurture of the Lord, and to the praise of his holy Name.

Secondly, It was ordained for a remedy against sin, and to avoid fornication; that such persons as have not the gift of continency might marry, and keep themselves undefiled members of Christ's body.

Thirdly, It was ordained for the mutual society, help, and comfort, that the one ought to have of the other, both in prosperity and adversity. Into which holy estate these two persons present come now to be joined. Therefore if any man can shew any just cause, why they may not lawfully be joined together, let him now speak, or else hereafter for ever hold his peace.

And also, speaking unto the persons that shall be married, he shall say,

I REQUIRE and charge you both, as ye will answer at the dreadful day of judgement when the secrets of all hearts shall be disclosed, that if either of you know any impediment, why ye may not be lawfully joined together in Matrimony, ye do now confess it. For be ye well assured, that so many as are coupled together otherwise than God's Word doth allow are not joined together by God; neither is their Matrimony lawful.

At which day of Marriage, if any man do alledge and declare any impediment, why they may not be coupled together in Matrimony, by God's Law, or the Laws of this Realm; and will be bound, and sufficient sureties with him, to the parties; or else put in a Caution (to the full value of such charges as the persons to be married do thereby sustain) to prove his allegation: then the solemnization must be deferred, until such time as the truth be tried.

If no impediment be alledged, then shall the Curate say unto the Man,
M. WILT thou have this Woman to thy wedded Wife, to live together after God's ordinance in the holy estate of Matrimony? Wilt thou love her, comfort her, honour, and keep her in sickness and in health; and, forsaking all other, keep thee only unto her, so long as ye both shall live?

The Man shall answer, I will.

Then shall the Priest say unto the Woman,
N. WILT thou have this Man to thy wedded

Husband, to live together after God's ordinance in the holy estate of Matrimony? Wilt thou obey him, and serve him, love, honour, and keep him in sickness and in health; and, forsaking all other, keep thee only unto him, so long as ye both shall live?

The Woman shall answer, I will.

Then shall the Minister say,
Who giveth this Woman to be married to this Man?

Then shall they give their troth to each other in this manner.

The Minister, receiving the Woman at her father's or friend's hands, shall cause the Man with his right hand to take the Woman by her right hand, and to say after him as followeth.

I M. take thee N. to my wedded Wife, to have and to hold from this day forward, for better for worse, for richer for poorer, in sickness and in health, to love and to cherish, till death us do part, according to God's holy ordinance; and thereto I plight thee my troth.

Then shall they loose their hands; and the Woman, with her right hand taking the Man by his right hand, shall likewise say after the

Minister,

I N. take thee M. to my wedded Husband, to have and to hold from this day forward, for better for worse, for richer for poorer, in sickness and in health, to love, cherish, and to obey, till death us do part, according to God's holy ordinance; and thereto I give thee my troth.

Then shall they again loose their hands; and the Man shall give unto the Woman a Ring, laying the same upon the book with the accustomed duty to the Priest and Clerk. And the Priest, taking the Ring, shall deliver it unto the Man, to put it upon the fourth finger of the Woman's left hand. And the Man holding the Ring there, and taught by the Priest, shall say,

WITH this Ring I thee wed, with my Body I thee worship, and with all my worldly Goods I thee endow: In the Name of the Father, and of the Son, and of the Holy Ghost. Amen.

Then the Man leaving the Ring upon the fourth finger of the Woman's left hand, they shall both kneel down, and the Minister shall say,

Let us pray.

O ETERNAL God, Creator and Preserver of all mankind, Giver of all spiritual grace, the

Author of everlasting life; Send thy blessing upon these thy servants, this Man and this Woman, whom we bless in thy Name; that, as Isaac and Rebecca lived faithfully together, so these persons may surely perform and keep the vow and covenant betwixt them made, (whereof this Ring given and received is a token and pledge,) and may ever remain in perfect love and peace together, and live according to thy laws; through Jesus Christ our Lord. Amen.

Then shall the Priest join their right hands together, and say,

Those whom God hath joined together let no man put asunder.

Then shall the Minister speak unto the people.

*F*ORASMUCH as M. and N. have consented together in holy Wedlock, and have witnessed the same before God and this company, and thereto have given and pledged their troth either to other, and have declared the same by giving and receiving of a Ring, and by joining of hands; I pronounce that they be Man and Wife together, In the Name of the Father, and of the Son, and of the Holy Ghost. Amen.

And the Minister shall add this Blessing.

GOD the Father, God the Son, God the Holy Ghost, bless, preserve, and keep you; the Lord mercifully with his favour look upon you; and so fill you with all spiritual benediction and grace, that ye may so live together in this life, that in the world to come ye may have life everlasting. Amen.

Then the Minister or Clerks, going to the Lord's Table, shall say or sing this Psalm following.

Beati Omnes Psalm 128.

BLESSED are all they that fear the Lord: and walk in his ways.

For thou shalt eat the labour of thine hands: O well is thee, and happy shalt thou be.

Thy wife shall be as the fruitful vine: upon the walls of thine house;
Thy children like the olive-branches: round about thy table.

Lo, thus shall the man be blessed: that feareth the Lord.

The Lord from out of Sion shall so bless

thee: that thou shalt see Jerusalem in prosperity all thy life long;

Yea, that thou shalt see thy children's children: and peace upon Israel.

Glory be to the Father, and to the Son: and to the Holy Ghost;

As it was in the beginning, is now, and ever shall be: world without end. Amen.

Or this Psalm

Deus misereatur Psalm 67.

GOD be merciful unto us, and bless us: and shew us the light of his countenance, and be merciful unto us.

That thy way may be known upon earth: thy saving health among all nations.

Let the people praise thee, O God: yea, let all the people praise thee.

O let the nations rejoice and be glad: for thou shalt judge the folk righteously, and govern the nations upon earth.

Let the people praise thee, O God: yea, let all the people praise thee.

Then shall the earth bring forth her increase: and God, even our own God, shall give us his blessing.

God shall bless us: and all the ends of the world shall fear him.

Glory be to the Father, and to the Son: and to the Holy Ghost;

As it was in the beginning, is now, and ever shall be: world without end. Amen

The Psalm ended, and the Man and the Woman kneeling before the Lord's Table, the Priest standing at the Table, and turning his face towards them, shall say,

Lord, have mercy upon us.

Answer. Christ, have mercy upon us.

Minister. Lord, have mercy upon us.

OUR Father, which art in heaven, Hallowed be thy Name. Thy kingdom come. Thy will be done in earth, As it is in heaven. Give us this day our daily bread. And forgive us our trespasses, As we forgive them that trespass against us. And lead us not into temptation; But deliver us from evil. Amen.

Minister. O Lord, save thy servant, and thy handmaid;

Answer. Who put their trust in thee.

Minister. O Lord, send them help from thy holy place;

Answer. And evermore defend them.
Minister. Be unto them a tower of strength,
Answer. From the face of their enemy.
Minister. O Lord, hear our prayer.
Answer. And let our cry come unto thee.
Minister.

O GOD of Abraham, God of Isaac, God of Jacob, bless these thy servants, and sow the seed of eternal life in their hearts; that whatsoever in thy holy Word they shall profitably learn, they may in deed fulfil the same. Look, O Lord, mercifully upon them from heaven, and bless them. And as thou didst send thy blessing upon Abraham and Sarah, to their great comfort, so vouchsafe to send thy blessing upon these thy servants; that they obeying thy will, and alway being in safety under thy protection, may abide in thy love unto their lives' end; through Jesus Christ our Lord. Amen.

This Prayer next following shall be omitted, where the Woman is past child-bearing.
O MERCIFUL Lord, and heavenly Father, by whose gracious gift mankind is increased; We beseech thee, assist with thy blessing these two persons, that they may both be fruitful in procreation of children, and also live together so long in godly love and honesty, that they may see their children christianly and virtu-

ously brought up, to thy praise and honour; through Jesus Christ our Lord. Amen.

O GOD, who by thy mighty power hast made all things of nothing; who also (after other things set in order) didst appoint, that out of man (created after thine own image and similitude) woman should take her beginning; and, knitting them together, didst teach that it should never be lawful to put asunder those whom thou by Matrimony hadst made one: O God, who hast consecrated the state of Matrimony to such an excellent mystery, that in it is signified and represented the spiritual marriage and unity betwixt Christ and his Church; Look mercifully upon these thy servants, that both this man may love his wife, according to thy Word, (as Christ did love his spouse the Church, who gave himself for it, loving and cherishing it even as his own flesh,) and also that this woman may be loving and amiable, faithful and obedient to her husband; and in all quietness, sobriety, and peace, be a follower of holy and godly matrons. O Lord, bless them both, and grant them to inherit thy everlasting kingdom; through Jesus Christ our Lord. Amen.

Then shall the Priest say,
ALMIGHTY God, who at the beginning did create our first parents, Adam and Eve, and

did sanctify and join them together in marriage; Pour upon you the riches of his grace, sanctify and bless you, that ye may please him both in body and soul, and live together in holy love unto your lives' end. Amen.

After which, if there be no Sermon declaring the Duties of Man and Wife, the Minister shall read as followeth.

ALL ye that are married, or that intend to take the holy estate of Matrimony upon you, hear what the holy Scripture doth say as touching the duty of husbands towards their wives, and wives towards their husbands.

Saint Paul, in his Epistle to the Ephesians, the fifth Chapter, doth give this commandment to all married men; Husbands, love your wives, even as Christ also loved the Church, and gave himself for it, that he might sanctify and cleanse it with the washing of water, by the Word; that he might present it to himself a glorious Church, not having spot, or wrinkle, or any such thing; but that it should be holy, and without blemish. So ought men to love their wives as their own bodies. He that loveth his wife loveth himself: for no man ever yet hated his own flesh, but nourisheth and cherisheth it, even as the Lord the Church: for we are members of his body, of his flesh, and of his bones. For this cause shall a man leave his father and mother, and shall be joined unto his wife; and they two shall be one flesh. This is a great mystery; but I speak concerning Christ and the Church. Nevertheless, let every one of you in particular so love his wife, even as himself.

Likewise the same Saint Paul, writing to the Colossians, speaketh thus to all men that are married; Husbands, love your wives, and be not bitter against them.

Hear also what Saint Peter, the Apostle of Christ, who was himself a married man, saith unto them that are married; Ye husbands, dwell with your wives according to knowledge; giving honour unto the wife, as unto the weaker vessel, and as being heirs together of the grace of life, that your prayers be not hindered.

Hitherto ye have heard the duty of the husband toward the wife. Now likewise, ye wives, hear and learn your duties toward your husbands, even as it is plainly set forth in holy Scripture.

Saint Paul, in the aforenamed Epistle to the Ephesians, teacheth you thus; Wives, submit yourselves unto your own husbands, as unto the Lord. For the husband is the head of the wife, even as Christ is the head of the Church: and he is the Saviour of the body. Therefore as the Church is subject unto Christ, so let the wives be to their own husbands in every thing. And again he saith, Let the wife see that she reverence her husband.

And in his Epistle to the Colossians, Saint Paul giveth you this short lesson; Wives, submit yourselves unto your own husbands, as it is fit in the Lord.

Saint Peter also doth instruct you very well, thus saying; Ye wives, be in subjection to your own husbands; that, if any obey not the Word, they also may without the Word be won by the conversation of the wives; while they behold your chaste conversation coupled with fear. Whose adorning, let it not be that outward adorning of plaiting the hair, and of wearing of gold, or of putting on of apparel; but let it be the hidden man of the heart, in that which is not corruptible; even the ornament of a meek and quiet spirit, which is in the sight of God of great price. For after this manner in the old time the holy women also, who trusted in God, adorned themselves, being in subjection unto their own husbands; even as Sarah obeyed Abraham, calling him lord; whose daughters ye are as long as ye do well, and are not afraid with any amazement.

It is convenient that the new-married persons should receive the holy Communion at the time of their Marriage, or at the first opportunity after their Marriage.

A Table of Kindred and Affinity

Wherein Whosoever Are Related Are Forbidden by the Church of England to Marry Together.

A Man may not marry his:	**A Woman may not marry with her:**
mother	father
daughter	son
adopted daughter	adopted son
father's mother	father's father
mother's mother	mother's father
son's daughter	son's son
daughter's daughter	daughter's son
sister	brother
wife's mother	husband's father
wife's daughter	husband's son
father's wife	mother's husband
son's wife	daughter's husband

father's father's wife	father's mother's husband
mother's father's wife	mother's mother's husband
wife's father's mother	husband's father's father
wife's mother's mother	husband's mother's father
wife's daughter's daughter	husband's son's son
wife's son's daughter	husband's daughter's son
son's son's wife	son's daughter's husband
daughter's son's wife	daughter's daughter's husband
father's sister	father's brother
mother's sister	mother's brother
brother's daughter	brother's son
sister's daughter	sister's son

In this Table the term 'brother' includes a brother of the half-blood, and the term 'sister' includes a sister of the half-blood.

From: The Book of Common Prayer, 1662

Lord Hardwicke's Marriage Act

An Act for the better preventing of clandestine Marriages

26 GEO II C 33

Whereas great Mischief and Inconveniencies Have arisen from Clandestine marriages, For preventing thereof for the future, Be it enacted by the King's most Excellent Majesty, by and with the Advice and Consent of the Lords Spiritual and Temporal, and Commons, in this present Parliament assembled, and by the Authority of the same, That from and after the twenty-fifth Day of March in the Year of our Lord one thousand seven hundred and fifty four, all Banns of Matrimony shall be published in an audible manner in the Parish

Church, or in some publick Chapel, in which publick Chapel Banns of Matrimony have been usually published, of or belonging to such Parish or Chapelry where in the persons to be married shall dwell, according to the form of the Words prescribed by the Rubrick prefixed to the Office of Matrimony in the Book of Common Prayer, upon three Sundays preceding the Solemnization of the marriage, during the time of Morning Service, or of Evening Service, (if there be no Morning Service in such Church or Chapel, upon those Sundays) immediately after the second lesson: and when soever it shall happen that the persons to be married shall dwell in divers Parishes or Chapelries, the banns shall in like manner be published in the Church or Chapel belonging to such parish or Chapelry wherein each of said persons shall dwell, and where both or either of the

Persons to be married shall dwell in any Extraparochial Place (having no Church or Chapel wherein Banns have been usually published) then the Banns shall in like manner be published in the parish Church or Chapel belonging to some Parish or Chapelry adjoining to such Extraparochial Place, the parson, Vicar, Minister, or Curate, publishing such Banns, shall in Writing, under his hand, certify the Publication thereof in such manner as if either of the persons to be married dwelt in such adjoining Parish; and that all other the Rules prescribed by the said Rubrick concerning the publication of the Banns, and the Solemnization of Matrimony, and not hereby altered, shall be duly observed, and that in all Cases where the Banns shall have been published, the Marriage shall be solemnized in one of the Parish churches or Chapels where such Banns have been published, and in no other Place whatsoever.

II

Provided always, and it is hereby further enacted, That no Parson, Vicar, Minister or Curate shall be obliged to publish the Banns of Matrimony between any Persons whatsoever, unless the Persons to be married shall seven Days at the least before the time required for the First Publication of such Banns respectively , deliver, or cause to be delivered to such Parson, Vicar, Minister, or Curate , a Notice in Writing of their true Christian and Surnames, and of the Houses or Houses of their respective Abodes, within such Parish, Chapelry, or Extraparochial Place, as aforesaid, and of the Time during which they have dwelt, inhabited or lodged in such House or Houses respectively.

III

Provided always , and be it enacted by the Authority aforesaid, that no Parson, Minister, Vicar or Curate solemnizing Marriages after the twenty -fifth Day of march one thousand seven hundred and fifty four, between persons both or one of whom shall be under age of twenty-one Years , after Banns published, shall be punishable by Ecclesiastical Censures for solemnizing such Marriages without Consent of Parents or Guardians, whose Consent is required by Law, unless such Parson, Minister, Vicar, or Curate shall have Notice of the Dissent of such Parents or Guardians; and in case such Parents or Guardians, or one of them , shall openly and publickly declare or cause to be declared in the Church or Chapel where the Banns shall be so published, at the Time of such Publication, his, her or their Dissent to such Marriage such Publication of banns shall be absolutely void.

IV

And it is hereby further enacted, that no Licence of marriage shall, from and after the said twenty-fifth day of March in the Year one thousand seven hundred and fifty-four, be granted by any Archbishop, Bishop, or other Ordinary or Person having authority to grant such Licences, to solemnize any Marriage in any other Church or Chapel, than in the parish Church or Publick Chapel of or belonging to the parish or Chapelry within which the usual Place of Abode of one of the Persons to be married shall have been for the space of four Weeks immediately before the granting of such Licence; or where both or either of the Parties to be married shall dwell in any Extraparochial Place, having no Church or Chapel belonging to some parish or Chapelry wherein Banns have usually been Published , adjoining to such Extraparochial Place, and in no other Place Whatsoever.

V

Provided always, that it be enacted by the Authority aforesaid, that all parties where there shall be no Parish Church or Chapel belonging thereto, or none wherein Divine Service shall be usually celebrated every Sunday , may be deemed Extraparochial Places for the Purposes of this Act but not for nay other Purpose.

VI

Provided always, That nothing herein contained shall be construed to extend to deprive the Archbishop of Canterbury and his Successors, and his and their proper Officers, of the Right which hath hitherto been used, in virtue of a certain Statute made in the twenty-fifth Year of the Reign of the Late King Henry the eighth, intituled An Act Concerning Peter

Pence and Dispensations, of granting Special licences to marry at any convenient Time and Place.

VII

Provided always, and be it enacted, That from and after the twenty-fifth day of March in the Year One thousand seven hundred and fifty-four, no Surrogate deputed by any Ecclesiastical Judge, who hath Power to grant Licences of Marriage, shall grant any such Licence before he hath taken an oath, before the said Judge faithfully to execute his Office, according to Law, to the best of his Knowledge, and hath given security by his Bond in the sum of one hundred Pounds to the Bishops of the Diocese, for the due and faithful Execution of said Office.

VIII

And whereas Many Parsons do Solemnize Matrimony in Prisons and other places without Publication of Banns, or Licence of marriage first being obtained; Therefore, for the Prevention thereof, Be it enacted ,That if any Person shall, from and after said twenty-fifth Day of March in the Year one thousand seven hundred fifty-four, solemnize Matrimony in any other Place than a Church or a Publick Chapel, where Banns have usually been published, unless by Special Licence from the Archbishop of Canterbury; or shall Solemnize Matrimony without Publication of Banns , unless Licence of Marriage be first had and obtained from some Person or Persons having Authority to grant the same, every Person knowingly and willfully so offending , and being lawfully convicted thereof, shall be deemed and adjudged guilty of Felony, and shall be transported to some of His Majesty's Plantations in America for the space of fourteen years, according to the Laws in Force for transportation of Felons; and all Marriages solemnized from and after the twenty-fifth day of March in the Year on thousand seven hundred and fifty-four, in any other Place than a Church or Publick Chapel, unless by Special License, as aforesaid, or that shall be solemnized without Publication of Banns, or License of Marriage from a Person, or Persons having Authority to grant the same first had and obtained, shall be null and void to all Intents and Purposes whatsoever.

IX

Provided that all Prosecutions for such Felony shall be commenced within the Space of three Years after the Offence committed.

X

Provided always that after the Solemnization of any Marriage under a Publication of Banns,

Proof shall not be necessary in support such
Marriages, to give any proof of the actual
Dwelling place of the Parties in the respective
Parishes or Chapelries wherein the Banns of
Matrimony were published; or where the
Marriage is by License, it shall not be neces-
sary to give any Proof that the usual Place of
Abode of one of the Parties, for the space of
Four Weeks, as aforesaid, was in the Parish or
Chapelry where the Marriage was solemnized,
nor shall any evidence in either of the said
Cases be received to prove the contrary in any
suit touching the validity of the Marriage.

XI

And it is hereby further enacted, That all Marriages Solemnized by a License after the said
twenty-fifth day of March , one thousand sev-
en hundred and fifty four, where either of the
Parties , not being Widower or Widow, shall
be under the Age of twenty-one Years, which
shall be had without the Consent of the father
of such Parties, so under Age (if then living)
first had and obtained, or if dead of the
Guardian or Guardians of the Person of the
Party so under Age, lawfully appointed, or one
of them; and in case there shall be no such
Guardian or Guardians, then of the Mother (
if living and unmarried) or if there shall be no
Mother living and Unmarried, then of a
Guardian or Guardians of the Person appoint-

ed by the Court of Chancery; shall be absolutely null and void to all Intents and Purposes whatsoever.

XII

And whereas it may happen that the Guardian or Guardians. Mother or Mothers, of the Parties to be married , or one of them, so under Age as aforesaid, may be non Compos mentis, or may be in Parts beyond the Seas, or shall refuse or with-hold his, her or their Consent to the Marriage of any Person, it shall and may be lawful for any Person desirous of marrying, in any of the before mentioned Cases, to apply by Petition to the Lord Chancellor, Lord Keeper, or the Lords Commissioners of the Great Seal of Great Britain for the Time Being who is and are hereby impowered to proceed upon such Petition, in a summary Way; and in Case the Marriage proposed shall upon Examination appear to be proper, the said Lord Chancellor, Lord Keeper, or the Lord Commissioners of the Great Seal for the Time being. shall judicially declare the same to be so by Order of Court, and such Order shall be deemed and taken to be as good and effectual to all intents and Purposes, as if the Guardian or Guardians, or Mother of the Person so petitioning had consented to such marriage.

XIII

And it is hereby further enacted, That in no Case whatsoever shall any Suit or Proceeding be had in any Ecclesiastical Court, in order to compel a Celebration of any Marriage in facie Ecclesie by reason of any Contract of Matrimony whatsoever, whether per verba de prasenti or per verba de future, which shall be entered into after the twenty-fifth day of March in the Year one thousand seven hundred and fifty-four, any Law or Usage to the contrary not withstanding.

XIV

And for preventing undue Entries and Abuses in Registers of Marriages ; Be it enacted by the Authority aforesaid, That on or before the twenty-fifth Day of March in the Year one thousand seven hundred and fifty-four, and from Time to Time afterwards as there shall be Occasion, the church -wardens and Chapel Wardens of every Parish and Chapelry shall provide proper Books of Vellum , or good and durable Paper, in which all Marriages and Banns of Marriages respectively, there published or solemnized , shall be registered , and every Page there of shall be marked at the Top with the figure of a Number of every such Page, beginning at the second Leaf with the number one , and every Leaf or page so numbered shall be ruled with Lines at proper and equal Distance from each other , or as near as conveniently may be to such ruled Lines, and shall be signed by the Parson, Vicar, Minister, or Curate, or by some other Person in his Presence and by his Direction; and such Entries shall be made as aforesaid on or near such Lines in successive Order where the Paper is not damaged or decayed , by Accident or Length of Time , until a new Book shall be thought proper or necessary to be provided for the same Purposes, and then the Directions aforesaid shall be observed in every new such Book; and all Books provided as aforesaid shall be deemed to belong to every such parish or Chapelry respectively, and shall be carefully kept and preserved for publick Use.

XV

And in order to preserve the Evidence of Marriages, and to make the Proof thereof more certain and easy and for the Direction of Ministers in the Celebration of Marriages and registering thereof, Be it enacted, That from and after the twenty-fifth day of march one thousand seven hundred and fifty-four, all marriages shall be solemnized in the presence of two or more credible Witnesses, besides the Minister who shall celebrate the same; and that immediately after the Celebration of every marriage, an Entry thereof shall be made in such Register to be kept as aforesaid; in which

Entry or Register it shall be expressed , That
the said marriage was celebrated by Banns or
Licence; and if both or either of the Parties
married by Licence be under age with Consent of the Parents or Guardians, as the Case
shall be, and shall be signed by the Minister
with his proper Addition, and also by the Parties married, and attested by such two
Witnesses, which entry shall be made in the
Form or to the Effect following: A.B of [the or
this] Parish and C.D. {of the of this] Parish
were married in this [Church, Chapel] by
Banns, Licence] with the Consent of [Parents ,
Guardians] this _____ Day of the Year
_____ by Name of officiating clergy followed by curate, vicar, rector. This Marriage
was solemnized between us A.B and CD. in
the presence of E.F and G.H. (and signed by
the bride and groom)

XVI

And be it further enacted by the authority
aforesaid, That if any person shall, from and
after twenty-fifth day of March in the Year
one thousand seven hundred fifty-four, with
Intent to elude the Force of this Act, knowingly and wilfully insert, or cause to be inserted
in the Register Book of such Parish or
Chapelry as aforesaid, any false Entry of any
Matter or Thing relating to any Marriage; or
falsely make, alter, forge, or counterfeit or

cause or procure to be falsely made, altered, forged or counterfeited, or act or assist in falsely making, altering, forging, or counterfeiting any such Entry in such Register; or falsely make, alter, forge or counterfeit, or cause or procure to be falsely made, altered, forged, or counterfeited, or assist in falsely making ,altering forging or counterfeiting any such Licence of Marriage as aforesaid; or utter or publish as true any such false, altered, forged, or counterfeited Register as aforesaid, or a Copy thereof; or any such false, altered, forged, or counterfeited Licence of Marriage , knowing such Register or Licence of Marriage respectively to be false, altered, forged or counterfeited; or if any Person shall, from and after the said twenty-fifth day of March, wilfully destroy or cause or procure to be destroyed, any Register Book of Marriages, or any Part of such Register Book, with Intent to avoid any Marriage, or to subject any Person to any of the Penalties of this Act; every Person so offending , and being thereof lawfully convicted, shall be deemed and adjudged to be guilty of a Felony, and shall suffer Death as a Felon, without Benefit of Clergy.

XVII

Provided always, That this Act, or any Thing therein contained, shall not extend to the Marriages of any of the Royal Family.

XVIII

Provided Likewise , That nothing in this Act contained shall extend to that part of Great Britain called Scotland, nor to any Marriages amongst the People called Quakers, or amongst the Persons professing the Jewish Religion, where both Parties to any such Marriage shall be of the People called Quakers, or Persons professing the Jewish Religion respectively, nor to any Marriage solemnized beyond the Seas.

XIX

And be it further enacted by the Authority aforesaid , That this Act shall be publickly read in all Parish Churches and Publick Chapels, by the Parson, Vicar, Minister or Curate of the respective Parishes or Chapelries on some Sunday immediately after Morning Prayer or immediately after Evening Prayer, if there shall be no Morning Service on that day in each of the Months of September, October, November, and December in the year one thousand seven fifty three, and afterwards at the same Times, on four several Sundays of the Year (that is to say) The Sundays next before the twenty-fifth Day of March, twenty fourth Day of June, twenty ninth day of September and the twenty-fifth Day of December respectively for two Years, to be computed from and immediately after the First Day of January in said Year one thousand seven hundred and fifty four.

APPENDIX D

An Early Wedding Cake Recipe

To make a Bride Cake.

TAKE four pounds of fine flour well dried, four pounds of fresh butter, two pounds of loaf sugar, pound and sift fine a quarter of an ounce of mace, the same of nutmegs, to every pound of flour put eight eggs, wash four pounds of currants, pick them well, and dry them before the fire, blanch a pound of sweet almonds, and cut them lengthways very thin, a pound of citron, one pound of candied orange, the same of candied lemon, half a pint of brandy; first work the butter with your hand to a cream, then beat in your sugar a quarter of an hour, beat the whites of your eggs to a very strong froth, mix them with your sugar and butter, beat your yolks half an hour at least, and mix them with your cake, then put in your flour, mace, and nutmeg, keep beating it well till your oven is ready, put in your brandy, and beat your currants and almonds lightly in, tie three sheets of paper round the bottom of your hoop to keep it from running out, rub it well with butter, put in your cake, and lay your sweetmeats in three lays, with cake betwixt every lay, after it is risen and coloured, cover it with paper before your oven is stopped up; it will take three hours baking.

To make Almond-icing for the Bride Cake.

BEAT the whites of three eggs to a strong froth, beat a pound of Jordan almonds very fine with rose-water, mix your almonds with the eggs lightly together, a pound of common loaf sugar, beat fine, and put in by degrees; when your cake is enough, take it out, and lay your icing on, then put it in to brown.

To make Sugar Icing for the Bride Cake.

BEAT two pounds of double refined sugar, with two ounces of fine starch, lift it through a gauze sieve, then beat the whites of five eggs with a knife upon a pewter dish half an hour; beat in your sugar a little at a time, or it will make the eggs fall, and will not be so good a colour, when you have put in all your sugar, beat it half an hour longer, then lay it on your almond icing, and spread it even with a knife; if it be put on as soon as the cake comes out of the oven it will be hard by the time the cake is cold.

(Raffald,1786)

Bibliography

Ackermann's Repository. March, 1818 series 2, Vol 5. Bridal Dress.

Ackermann's Repository of Arts, Literature, Commerce, Manufactures, Fashion and Politics. June 1816. 'Bridal dress'.

Adkins, Roy, and Lesley Adkins. *Jane Austen's England.* Viking, 2013.

Allen, Louise. "Banns or Licence? Ways To Marry in Georgian England." Jane Austens London. May 7, 2014. Accessed July 24,2016 https://janeaustenslondon.com/2014/05/07/banns-or-licence-ways-to-marry-in-georgian-england/

Austen, Jane, and David M. Shapard. *The Annotated Pride and Prejudice.* New York: Anchor Books, 2003.

Austen, Jane, and David M. Shapard. *The Annotated Sense and Sensibility.* New York: Anchor Books, 2011.

Austen, Jane, and Laura Engel. *Sense and Sensibility.* New York: Barnes & Noble Classics, 2003.

Austen, Jane, and Margaret Drabble. *Emma.* New York, NY: Signet Classic, 1996.

Austen, Jane, and Pat Rogers. *Pride and Prejudice*. Cambridge: Cambridge University Press, 2006.

Austen, Jane, Claude Julien. Rawson, and John Davie. *Persuasion*. Oxford: Oxford University Press, 1990.

Austen, Jane, Marilyn Butler, and James Kinsley. *Mansfield Park*. Oxford: Oxford University Press, 1990.

Austen, Jane, Terry Castle, and John Davie. *Northanger Abbey ; Lady Susan ; The Watsons ; Sanditon*. Oxford: Oxford University Press, 1990.

Austen, Jane. *Pride and Prejudice*. New York: Tor, 1988.

Austen-Leigh, Mary Augusta. *Personal Aspects of Jane Austen*. London: J. Murray, 1920.

Bailey, Joanne. *Unquiet Lives: Marriage and Marriage Breakdown in England 1660-1800.* Cambridge: Cambridge University Press, 2003.

Baird, Rosemary. *Mistress of the House: Great Ladies and Grand Houses, 1670-1830.* London: Phoenix, 2004.

Banche, Linda. "Historical Hussies." : Eloping in Regency England. August 19, 2009. Accessed November 23, 2015.

http://historicalhussies.blogspot.com/2009/08/eloping-in-regency-england.html.

Barreto, Cristina, and Martin Lancaster. *Napoleon and the Empire of Fashion, 1795-1815*. Milan: Skira, 2010.

Bates, Denise. "Breach of Promise to Marry Research - Facts and Figures." Denise Bates. July 14, 2016. Accessed Aug 10, 2016. http://www.denisebates.co.uk/bopfacts.html

Bates, Denise. "Breach of Promise to Marry Research – New Discoveries." Denise Bates. October 3, 2015. Accessed Aug 10, 2016. http://www.denisebates.co.uk/bopdiscoveries.html

Bennett, John. *Letters to a Young Lady, on a Variety of Useful and Interesting Subjects Calculated to Improve the Heart, to Form the Manners and Enlighten the Understanding. "That Our Daughters May Be as Polished Corners of the Temple."* 6th American ed. Hudson: Printed by William E Norman, 1811.

Blackstone, William. *Commentaries on the Laws of England.* Vol, 1 (1765), pages 442-445.

Brother, Younger, B. M----n, and B. M---n. *A Master-key to the Rich Ladies Treasury; Or, The Widower and Batchelor's Directory.* London: J. Roberts, 1742.

Bullough, Vern L., and Bonnie Bullough. *Prostitution: An Illustrated Social History*. New York: Crown Publishers, 1978.

Child, Lydia Maria. *The Girl's Own Book*. New York: Clark Austin &, 3 Park Row & 3 Ann-St., 1833.

Collins, Irene. *Jane Austen and the Clergy*. London: Hambledon and London, 2001.

Collins, Irene. *Jane Austen, the Parson's Daughter*. London: Hambledon Press, 1998.

Corbould, Edward Henry. *The Young Lady's Own Book a Manual of Intellectual Improvement and Moral Deportment*. Philadelphia: Key & Biddle, 1834.

Davidoff, Leonore, and Catherine Hall. *Family Fortunes: Men and Women of the English Middle Class, 1780-1850*. Chicago: University of Chicago Press, 1987.

Day, Malcom. *Voices from the World of Jane Austen*. David&Charles, 2006.

Eakes, Laurie Alice. "An Alternative Elopement." Vanessa Rileys Christian Regency Blog. June 25, 2012. Accessed November 23, 2015. http://christianregency.com/blog/2012/06/2 5/laurie-alice-alternative-elopement/.

Erickson, Amy Louise. *Women and Property in Early Modern England*. London: Routledge, 1993.

Flinders, M. Gratefull to providence: *The diary and accounts of Matthew Flinders, surgeon, apothecary and man-midwife, 1775–1802: Vol. 1: 1775–1784.* Ed. Martyn Beardsley and Nicholas Bennett. Lincoln Record Society, United Kingdom, 2008.

Forsling, Yvonne . "Regency Weddings: Fashion Periodicals." Hibiscus-Sinensis. Accessed July 22, 2016. http://hibiscus-sinensis.com/regency/weddingprints.htm

Forsling, Yvonne. "Weddings During the Regency." Jane Austen. June 20, 2011. Accessed July 24, 2016. https://www.janeausten.co.uk/weddings-during-the-regency-era/

Fullerton, Susannah. *Jane Austen and Crime.* Sydney: Jane Austen Society of Australia, 2004.

Gatrell, Vic. *City of Laughter: Sex and Satire in Eighteenth-century London*. New York: Walker &, 2007.

Gener, S., and John Muckersy. *M. Gener, Or, A Selection of Letters on Life and Manners*. 3rd ed. Edinburgh: Printed for Peter Hill ..., A. Constable & and A. MacKay ;, 1812.

Girouard, Mark. *Life in the English Country House: A Social and Architectural History.* New Haven: Yale University Press, 1978.

Gisborne, Thomas. *An Enquiry into the Duties of the Female Sex.* London: Cadell and Davies, 1797.

Gregory, John. *A Father's Legacy to His Daughters By the Late Dr. Gregory, of Edinburgh.* The 2nd ed. London: Printed for W. Strahan ;, 1774.

Gronow, R. H., and C. J. Summerville. *Regency Recollections: Captain Gronow's Guide to Life in London and Paris.* Welwyn Garden City, U.K.: Ravenhall, 2006.

Hager, Kelly. "Chipping Away at Coverture: The Matrimonial Causes Act of 1857." BRANCH: Britain, Representation and Nineteenth-Century History. Ed. Dino Franco Felluga. Extension of Romanticism and Victorianism on the Net. Web. [Accessed 7/29/16]. http://www.branchcollective.org/?ps_articles =kelly-hager-chipping-away-at-coverture- the-matrimonial-causes-act-of-1857.

Harvey, A. D. *Sex in Georgian England: Attitudes and Prejudices from the 1720s to the 1820s.* New York: St. Martin's Press, 1994.

Heydt-Stevenson, Jillian *Austen's Unbecoming Conjunctions: Subversive Laughter, Embodied History.* New York: Palgrave Macmillan, 2005

Horstman, Allen. *Victorian Divorce.* New York: St. Martin's Press, 1985.

Jones, Hazel. *Jane Austen and Marriage.* London: Continuum, 2009.

Jones, J.W. *A Translation of all the Greek, Latin, Italian and French Quotations which occur in Blackstone's Commentaries on the Laws of England.* Philadelphia: T7JW Johnson&Co. 1905. Accessed August 5, 2015. http://www.mindserpent.com/American_History/books/Blackstone/trans_01.htm.

Kane, Kathryn. "Marriage Lines" really are lines!_Regency Redingote. 19 December 2008 Accessed December 23, 2015. https://regencyredingote.wordpress.com/2008/12/19/marriage-lines-really-are-lines/

Kelly, Ian. *Beau Brummell: The Ultimate Man of Style.* New York: Free Press, 2006.

Koster, Kristen. "A Regency Primer on Annulment and Divorce." Kristen Koster. October 18, 2011. Accessed January 15, 2016. http://www.kristenkoster.com/2011/10/a-regency-divorce-primer/.

La Belle Assemblee. October 1819. Parisian Evening Bridal Dress .

Lane, Allison.. *Common Regency Errors.* Oct 11, 2014 http://web.archive.org/web/20141011193636 /http://www.eclectics.com:80/allisonlane/co mmon_regency_errors.html   Accessed 12/15/16

Lane, Maggie. *Jane Austen's World: The Life and times of England's Most Popular Novelist.* 2nd ed. London: Carlton Books, 2005.

Laudermilk, Sharon H., and Teresa L. Hamlin. *The Regency Companion.* New York: Garland, 1989.

LeFaye, Deirdre. *Jane Austen: The World of Her Novels.* New York: Abrams, 2002.

Lewis, Jone Johnson. "Blackstone Commen- taries: Women and the Law." Womens History. March 12, 2016. Accessed May 5, 2016. http://womenshistory.about.com/cs/lives19th /a/blackstone_law.htm

Lewis, Judith Schneid. *In the Family Way: Childbearing in the British Aristocracy, 1760- 1860.* New Brunswick, N.J.: Rutgers Universi- ty Press, 1986.

M.,Y. *Some Remarks on Matrimonial Advertise- ments Being an Inquiry into their Use and Abuse.* London: Sedding and Turtle, 1832.

Macfarlane, Alan. *Marriage and Love in England: Modes of Reproduction 1300-1840.* New York: Basil Blackwel, Inc., 1986.

"Marriage Settlements in England and Wales." Genealogy. February 3, 2016. Accessed March 23, 2016. https://familysearch.org/wiki/en/Marriage_S ettlements_in_England_and_Wales.

Martin, Joanna. *Wives and Daughters: Women and Children in the Georgian Country House.* London: Hambledon and London, 2004.

Matthews, Mimi. "Alternative Courtship: Matrimonial Advertisements in the 19th Century." Mimi Matthews. January 04, 2016. Accessed January 4, 2016. https://mimimatthews.com/2016/01/04/alter native-courtship-matrimonial-advertisements-in-the-19th-century/.

Mayer, Nancy. "Dissolving a Marriage." Regency Researcher. Accessed November 3, 2015. http://www.regencyresearcher.com/pages/m arriagedis.html

Mayer, Nancy. "Hardwicke Act." Regency Researcher. Accessed November 3, 2015. http://www.regencyresearcher.com/pages/m arriagedis.html

Mayer, Nancy. "Marriage." Regency Researcher. Accessed November 3, 2015. http://www.regencyresearcher.com/pages/m arriagedis.html

"Mr. Beveridge's Maggot". Regency Dances. Accessed August 1, 2016. http://regencydances.org/index.php?wL=153

Mullan, John. "Courtship, love and marriage in Jane Austen's novels." British Library. Accessed July 26, 2016. http://www.bl.uk/romantics-and-victorians/articles/courtship-love-and-marriage-in-jane-austens-novels#sthash.R9ucg3zh.dpuf

Murray, Venetia. *An Elegant Madness: High Society in Regency England*. New York: Viking, 1999.

Parkes, William. *Domestic Duties: Or, Instructions to Young Married Ladies*. London: Longman, Hurst, Rees, Orme, Brown and Green, 1825.

Perkin, Jane. *Women and Marriage in Nineteenth-Century England. London*: Routledge, 1989.

Perry, Ruth. *Sleeping with Mr. Collins PERSUASIONS NO. 22 (2000)* Pages 119-135.

Raffald, Elizabeth. *The Experienced English Housekeeper for the Use and Ease of Ladies,*

Housekeepers, Cooks, &c. Written Purely from Practice ... Consisting of near Nine Hundred Original Receipts, Most of Which Never Appeared in Print. ... The Tenth Edition. ... By Elizabeth Raffald. London: Printed for R. Baldwin, 1786.

Ray, Joan Klingel. *Jane Austen for Dummies*. Chichester: John Wiley, 2006.

Reeves-Brown, Jessamyn. Regency Wedding Details & History, 2004. Accessed July 25, 2016. http://www.songsmyth.com/weddings.html.

"Regency Wrangles." : Georgian & Regency Divorce. April 25, 2010. Accessed December 23, 2015. http://regencywrangles.blogspot.com/2010/04/georgian-regency-divorce.html.

Rendell, Jane. *The Pursuit of Pleasure Gender, Space & Architecture in Regency London*. London: Athlone Press, 2002.

Ross, Josephine, and Henrietta Webb. *Jane Austen's Guide to Good Manners: Compliments, Charades & Horrible Blunders*. New York: Bloomsbury USA, 2006.

Sanborn, Vic. "A Master Key to the Rich Ladies Treasury: The Marriage Mart in Georgian England." Jane Austens World. February 22, 2012. Accessed December 23, 2015. https://janeaustensworld.wordpress.com/201

2/02/22/a-master-key-to-the-rich-ladies-treasury/.

Sanborn, Vic. "And the Bride Wore..." Jane Austen. June 17, 2011. Accessed July 25, 2016 https://www.janeausten.co.uk/and-the-bride-wore/.

Sanborn, Vic. "The London Season: A Marriage Mart." Jane Austens World. August 30, 2006 Accessed January 12, 2016. https://janeaustensworld.wordpress.com/2006/08/30/the-london-season-a-marriage-mart/

Sanborn, Vic. "The Marriage Mart: A Romantic Ending to an Unromantic Beginning." Jane Austens World. July 6, 2008 Accessed January 12, 2016. https://janeaustensworld.wordpress.com/2008/07/06/the-marriage-mart-a-romantic-ending-to-an-unromantic-beginning/

Sanborn, Victoria. "Dowagers and Widows in 19th C. England." Jane Austens World. Sept 14, 2011. Accessed December 5, 2015. http://janeaustensworld.wordpress.com/2011/09/14/dowagers-and-widows-in-19th-c-england/

Savage, William . "Hapless Husbands and Wandering Wives." Pen and Pension. June 29, 2016. Accessed June 29, 2016.

https://penandpension.com/2016/06/29/hapl
ess-husbands-and-wandering-wives/ .

Savage, William. "Marriage amongst the Mid-
dling Sort." Pen and Pension. June 22, 2016.
Accessed June 22, 2016.
https://penandpension.com/2016/06/22/mar
riage-amongst-the-middling-sort/.

Selwyn, David. *Jane Austen and Leisure*. London: Hambledon Press, 1999.

Shoemaker, Robert Brink. *Gender in English
Society, 1650-1850: The Emergence of Separate
Spheres?* London: Longman, 1998. Pearson
Education Limited

Stone, Lawrence. *Broken Lives: Separation and
Divorce in England 1660-1857*. Oxford University Press, 1993.

Stone, Lawrence. *The Family, Sex and Marriage
in England, 1500-1800*. New York: Harper &
Row, 1979.

Stone, Lawrence. *The Road to Divorce: England
1530-1987*. Oxford: Oxford University Press,
1990.

Stone, Lawrence. *Uncertain Unions: Marriage in
England 1660-1753*. Oxford: Oxford University
Press, 1992.

Sullivan, Margaret C., and Kathryn Rathke.
The Jane Austen Handbook: Proper Life Skills

from Regency England. Philadelphia, PA: Quirk Books, 2007.

Taylor, Ann. *Practical Hints to Young Females: On the Duties of a Wife, a Mother, and a Mistress of a Family.* 10th ed. London: Taylor and Hessey, 1822.

The Book of Common Prayer and Administration of the Sacraments and Other Rites and Ceremonies of the Church, According to the Use of the Church of England: Together with the Psalter or Psalms of David, Pointed as They Are to Be Sung or Said in Churches: The Form and Manner of Making, Ordaining, and Consecrating of Bishops, Priests, and Deacons. Cambridge: Printed by John Field, 1662.

The Whole Duty of a Woman, Or, an Infallible Guide to the Fair Sex. Containing, Rules, Directions, and Observations, for Their Conduct and Behaviour through All Ages and Circumstances of Life, as Virgins, Wives, or Widows. With Directions, How to Obtain All Use. The 2nd ed. London: Printed for T. Read, in Dogwell-Court, White-Fryers, Fleet-Street, 1737.

The Young Husband's Book a Manual of the Duties, Moral, Religious, and Domestic, Imposed by the Relations of Married Life. Philadelphia: Lea & Blanchard, 1839.

Trevelyan, George Macaulay. *Illustrated English Social History.* New York: D. McKay, 1949.

Vickery, Amanda. *Behind Closed Doors: At Home in Georgian England*. New Haven, Conn.: Yale University Press, 2009.

Vickery, Amanda. *The Gentleman's Daughter: Women's Lives in Georgian England*. New Haven, Conn.: Yale University Press, 1998.

Watkins, Susan. *Jane Austen's Town and Country Style*. New York: Rizzoli, 1990.

Wilson, Ben. *The Making of Victorian Values: Decency and Dissent in Britain, 1789-1837*. New York: Penguin Press, 2007.

Wilson, Carol. Gastronomica: The Journal Of Food And Culture, vol. 5, no. 2, pp. 69–72, issn 1529-3262.

Woodley, Anne. "Regency Life - Marriage." Regency Life - Marriage. Accessed March 23, 2016. http://homepages.ihug.co.nz/~awoodley/regency/legalwomen.html.

Wright, Danaya C. "Well-Behaved Women Don't Make History": *Rethinking English Family, Law, and History*, 19 Wis. Women's L.J. 211 2004), August 17, 2012. Accessed August 1, 2016. http://scholarship.law.ufl.edu/facultypub/128

Index

Acknowledgments

So many people have helped me along the journey taking this from an idea to a reality.

Debbie, Julie, and Anji thank you so much for cold reading and being honest; your proofreading is worth your weight in gold!

Abigail, my writing buddy, sounding board, and overall support. I can't tell you how much I love working with you.

My dear friend Cathy, my biggest cheerleader, you have kept me from chickening out more than once!

And my sweet sister Gerri who believed in even those first attempts that now live in the file drawer!

Thank you!

Other Books by Maria Grace

Available in paperback, e-book, and audiobook format at all online bookstores.

On Line Exclusives at:

RandomBitsofFascination.com

Bonus and deleted scenes
Regency Life Series

Free e-books:
Bits of Bobbin Lace
The Scenes Jane Austen Never Wrote: First Anniversaries
Half Agony, Half Hope: New Reflections on Persuasion
Four Days in April
Jane Bennet in January
February Aniversaries

About the Author

Though Maria Grace has been writing fiction since she was ten years old, those early efforts happily reside in a file drawer and are unlikely to see the light of day again, for which many are grateful. After penning five file-drawer novels in high school, she took a break from writing to pursue college and earn her doctorate in Educational Psychology. After 16 years of university teaching, she returned to her first love, fiction writing.

She has one husband, two graduate degrees and two black belts, three sons, four undergraduate majors, five nieces, six new novels in the works, attended seven period balls, sewn eight Regency era costumes, shared her life with nine cats through the years and published her tenth book in 2015.

Contact her at:

author.MariaGrace@gmail.com

Facebook:
http://facebook.com/AuthorMariaGrace

On Amazon.com:
http://amazon.com/author/mariagrace

Random Bits of Fascination
RandomBitsofFascination.com

Austen Variations (http://AustenVariations.com)

English Historical Fiction Authors
http://EnglshHistoryAuthors.blogspot.com)

White Soup Press whitesouppress.com/

On Twitter @WriteMariaGrace

On Pinterest:
http://pinterest.com/mariagrace423/

Printed in Great Britain
by Amazon